# HAPPINESS

# Cleaning

## How to Embrace the Mess and Love the Cleanup

**AURIKATARIINA KANANEN**

**OONA LAINE**

**NEA JOHANNA**

**mango**
PUBLISHING GROUP

CORAL GABLES

Cover & Layout Design: Megan Werner
Cover Photo: Hanna Tarkiainen
Interior Photos: Hanna Tarkiainen and Aurikatariina Kananen
Interior Illustrations: ADELART / stock.adobe.com

For permission requests, please contact the publisher at:
Mango Publishing Group
2850 S Douglas Road, 2nd Floor
Coral Gables, FL 33134 USA
info@mango.bz

For special orders, quantity sales, course adoptions and corporate sales,
please email the publisher at sales@mango.bz. For trade and wholesale
sales, please contact Ingram Publisher Services at customer.service@
ingramcontent.com or +1.800.509.4887.

Happiness Cleaning: How to Embrace the Mess and Love the Cleanup

Library of Congress Cataloging-in-Publication number: 2023943724
ISBN: (pb) 978-1-68481-333-9 (e) 978-1-68481-334-6
BISAC category code: HOM019000, HOUSE & HOME / Cleaning,
Caretaking & Organizing

Printed in the United States of America

# Table of Contents

# INTRODUCTION BY AURI

Hello dear reader,

You're holding a book that's sure to revolutionize your idea of cleaning. That's because behind the ideas in this book is me, Auri Kananen, the best cleaner in the world. You may know me better as Auri Katariina, the woman who cleans strangers' homes for free.

I'm originally from Finland, but my work in cleaning has flown me to conquer the entire planet. I've cleaned homes all over the world. I've been in the US numerous times as well, but I wish I could go there even more frequently! Once I even cleaned the Hollywood Walk of Fame.

Even though my videos on social media are watched by millions of people, few people really know me. *What kind of person is a woman in her thirties who would rather go cleaning than eat at a fancy restaurant, party, or enjoy a day at the spa?* Well, kind of like me. But I am much more than that, and I will tell you all about it unfiltered in the pages of this book.

You may be surprised, even sad, but most of all, I hope that I can inspire you and create hope for the future, even if it is difficult at the moment.

Since I'm not a writer but a cleaner (and I'd rather have a cleaning cloth in my hand than a pen), I had to think about finding the time for it. How could it be written? One day in January 2021, a reporter arrived at my home and seemed to have the job under control.

She knew how to ask the right questions and quickly figured out what kind of gal I really am. I realized it could be her. I thought she would probably see what this thing of mine is all about and be able to translate it as a clear story inside the covers of the book. Thank you, Oona, for becoming a travel guide to my wonderful world of cleaning!

I will be very happy if you, reader, enjoy the cleaning trip with me. I want to believe that this work will change your attitude toward home, dirt, and disorder. To change your perspective about cleaning as a tedious and distressing chore. Warning: It may happen that for you, like me, cleaning becomes a beloved hobby, a way of life, and something you really look forward to!

Joy for your cleaning days,

*Auri*

# A NOTE FROM THE AUTHOR

I'm Oona Laine, the author of this book. If someone had told me two years ago that I was going to write a book about a world-famous cleaning diva, I would have burst into laughter. It would have seemed like such an unreal idea at the time.

But here I am, thanks to my profession. I work as a journalist for *Helsingin Sanomat*, the largest newspaper in the Nordic countries. I have written a lot about home, living, and therefore cleaning. That doesn't mean that keeping my home organized and clean has interested me one bit. Quite the opposite: I've always been one of those girls who procrastinate until they finally grab the vacuum cleaner and start putting things in place. And then, when home has started to resemble a landfill again, anxiety comes over me. Why doesn't this just stay in shape?!

However, chance or fate led me to visit Auri and her then-fiancé Sam in January 2021. I had been hired to write a story about a much-loved, embarrassed cleaner who had become a world star in no time. We wanted to know how she herself lives.

Although I tried to avoid prejudice, I cannot deny that it existed. I expected to be met by a woman who would tell me to take off my shoes in the hallway and would wipe the table as soon as we got up. A woman whose every closet would be in perfect harmony. But, well, I was faced with a completely different case. An enthusiast bouncing from place to place who hadn't had the energy to make the bed, because it didn't bother her that much. The girl who immediately blurted out at the top of the interview that she would get mad at Sami if he cleaned while she was on a business trip or otherwise away from home. I listened to her with my ears red, shocked at first, until finally, when I left the gig, I noticed something else: I was inspired.

I was immensely inspired by the peculiar attitude to life that shone through her. She had the kind of relaxed attitude that I didn't have a drop of. I remember sharing Auri's "true nature" with everyone who could listen. By the way, the story about the gig was widely read, and I'm not surprised at all.

When a Finnish publishing company contacted me a couple of months later, I fell off my chair. Would I be the author of Auri's cleaning love book? *Surely not*, I thought, swallowing. But quite suddenly I replied, "Of course I agree!" It didn't take long for us to sit together again, this time in the publishing house, Auri in an all-pink outfit and me a little less colorful.

That was the beginning of the adventure that has given birth to this book. Among other things, the book has taken me to cleaning gigs in catastrophic locations and to ask Auri many small things, sometimes face to face, sometimes on the phone, sometimes just through messages. The best way to get the most out of Auri is when she has sent me voice messages.

At minimum, our relationship has resembled the contact between two friends.

And did anything change in me when the book was finished? Am I still a mildly negative person about cleaning, preferring to do anything but clean? You will find out by reading this book! Welcome, join us!

# PROLOGUE:
# FIRST THINGS FIRST

"Wonderful!"

What is?

In this story, many unusual things turn out to be wonderful. One of them is the floor of a shabby studio apartment. Well, actually, you can't be sure if there even is a floor. And if there is, it is covered in pizza boxes, bottles, overflowing plastic bags, and other unidentified stuff and junk. The stale-smelling sea of waste rises to waist height in certain places. Would such a floor be wonderful to you?

Do you know those stark reality TV shows that sensationalize chaotic homes? Homes in which the residents haven't seen daylight in months. The ones we stare at in disbelief, reassuring ourselves that there is no way homes like that exist, at least not in our neighborhood. This floor, and the home that is made on the floor, in the foyer of which I am now huddling, indeed reminds me of those television programmes with destroyed apartments and miserable human tragedies.

For the woman with me, the floor of that apartment is indeed wonderful. To get there, she traveled in her tiny van for hours, stopping at a gas station to pick up a box of tea bags as she usually does on these trips. She also booked a room for herself in the nearest hotel.

She never ceases to hum as she wades through the apartment and makes her way through the hallway bulging with stuff to the cramped alcove that is the bedroom. There lies the bed's worn-out mattress, which is about to drown among the piles of garbage. The woman looks at the poor mattress like it's a dear old friend.

She has her naturally blonde hair in two pigtails, a pink apron to protect her black clothes, and thick-soled glitter boots, which are pink of course. The glittery shoes would fit on the floor of a stylish night club, which is not too sticky because it gets scrubbed. Here, the boots do not stomp on the floor but rustle, thanks to the plastic, cardboard, and other matter suitable for compost carpeting it. It's like we're on a day trip in a sea of waste, and not on the second floor of a red-brick apartment building. The woman peeks into the bathroom, which is grimy, meaning

wonderful. She hums, nearly skips forward, until she gets tired of inaction and decides: *I've had enough.*

For starters, she and I pick up cleaning supplies from the van. We come across a cleaner wiping the staircase; their visit leaves the stairwell with the fresh scent of detergent. From the trunk of the car, we grab a ski box with cleaning extension arms. The plastic bucket contains a dish brush, garbage bags, and spray bottles. In the briefcase, there are towels scythed into a tidy bundle.

*There is an absolutely insane amount of cleaning stuff,* I can't help but think with wonder. At the same time, I send silent greetings to the past: to a brown-colored, mildly stinking rag that served me faithfully for years living alone. I remember how I dumped it unwashed and relentlessly into the closet among my vacuum cleaner, a mop, and a bunch of empty spray bottles. As my cleaning companion and I carry cleaning supplies to the stairwell, I get the feeling that the inside of her cleaning cupboard has never looked the same as mine.

When, after a painfully long time, she has captured the pre-cleaning situation on video, we put on pink rubber gloves. Then we get down to work that I don't think will see its conclusion in less than a week.

For the next few hours, we tear open dozens of garbage bags. I keep the mouth of the bag wide so that she can throw trash inside at her frenzied pace.

We start at the doorway, from where we proceed to every corner of the studio apartment. When there are five or six full garbage bags, we hurl them into the garbage bins outside and go back inside to fill new ones. It's like a rite that at first makes you gag because of the smell, but to which you become numb and accustomed. The nature of it leaves you hooked after the initial shock.

First, we come across paper, glossy magazines and some more fragile newspapers. The hallway is dominated by takeout boxes and containers, and bottles and cans that are resting empty on loose garbage as if they were left from a house party. Then I realize that I'm surrounded mostly by sugar-free soda cans and alcohol is represented only by a green glass bottle, a discarded canned cocktail, and a half-drunk bottle of wine. The floor is mostly flooded with pizza boxes with the crusts left uneaten. Beneath the piles of rubbish, there are packets and more takeout boxes, some of which still have the bones of chicken wings, wrapped in mold. We encounter blackened yellow capsicums, rotten bananas, and rock-hard oranges. They tumble into garbage bags like tennis balls hitting the court.

At the foot of the bed, and in many other corners, there are half-empty tubes of condiments, including mayonnaise and ketchup. In the bathroom, pickle jars are piled on top of the washing machine—inside the liquid-filled bottles float some lonely mystery items, but no actual pickles are in sight. From the floor of the shower, she picks up a moldy packet of hot dogs. She makes the same discovery in the fridge that also has hardened, skinned cherry tomatoes and portions of food shivering in gauze-like white mold.

They may have been chicken and rice in their previous lives, but I am not too sure. In particular, chewing gum is everywhere and stuck in places where you wouldn't think you'd come across it. On the walls and on the floor, glued to the edge of dirty plates, on the sides of empty bottles, under the rim of the toilet, and under the microwave.

From the middle of the waste, we can see some everyday stuff peeking through. This reminds us that we are cleaning the home of an actual living person. We can call him Oskar, who is perhaps thirty-something, and quietly and comfortably lives here. He met us in the yard, handing us the keys to his apartment. When my cleaning companion handed him the filming agreement to sign and he mumbled under his breath, he was doubting whether he could hold a pen in his hands anymore. That's how long it had been since he'd had to write.

"This looks really good, I can make sense of it," she assured him of his writing. Then we made our way back inside. Oskar's next-door neighbor opened his door and said with warmth in his voice: "Yes, it's just so good that you came here."

Now, however, Oskar is somewhere else until we are done here. Still, during the gig, I kind of got to know him. For example, it dawns on me that he loves Disney movies. There are hundreds of movies in the apartment. Some lie on the floor; some are lined up next to the TV.

We also find garbage-flooded electronics, such as an Apple watch, a Samsung phone, and some AirPods. There are also various medicine packages which we collect, in addition to videotapes and cassettes. When enough trash has been cleared, we realize the existence of a coffee table and a sofa. The first few hours, I would verbally let the shock come out of my mouth, but now I am quite speechless.

Finally, we are able to see the floor. At the end of the first four-hour effort, the layout of the apartment begins to stand out. It turns out that the floor is covered with a gray plastic mat. It's still clumped in dirt and full of crumbs and loose debris, but it's visible, probably for the first time in years.

We end up cleaning the apartment in two days, about eight hours each, including lunch breaks. We put dishwashing liquid on every surface and move things around and rearrange them. We scrape off the jars and snuff bags stuck in the bathroom sink. We empty the fridge, which in an instant she will make shine.

At noon, we stopped to eat: the first day on the terrace of a salad restaurant nearby, the second day at the salad buffet of a nearby grocery store. We inhaled the portions in the front seat of the van in the parking lot and watched the people walking past us. On the same trip, we went to get new sheets for Oskar's bed and a plant that we placed on top of the washing machine. The alcove with its mattress has become a cute booth that I could curl up in after this cleaning gig.

Finally, we are ready, and close the door so that Oskar can go back in peace. I can't help but wonder if he still recognizes the apartment as his own. We did not get the chance to see him before we left, so we can only hope our work helped him in some way.

When we finally sit on the train on our way to Helsinki, I'm in need of a hot shower, because I feel a little broken. But the lady in pink has already made plans to clean another apartment on the other side of Finland. She has been doing this, on average, once a week, for almost two years. She offers her help to ordinary people whose homes have gotten into such a state that the residents don't have the energy to clean them up themselves.

But the woman cleans them up, for free actually, and asks for one reward: permission to film a video of her cleaning.

The woman's name is Auri Kananen. Until a couple of years ago, Auri was a cleaner from Tampere, unknown to the general public. Nowadays, there aren't that many Finns who haven't heard of Auri.

"Is Auri Kananen, 27, the next Finnish superstar?" wondered *Yle*, Finland's national broadcasting network, in the title of an article published December 2020. The headline wasn't exactly on the wrong track, as in the same year the *British Daily Mail* had already had time to marvel at the extraordinary cleaning character: "Self-proclaimed 'best cleaner in the world' becomes a TikTok sensation with videos of her scrubbing dirty houses—and loves it so much she does it for free."

Then fast-forward to March 2022, when the international Italian women's magazine *Anna* flashed this fanciful headline: "Auri Kananen cleans other people's homes for free, and is therefore the best thing that has happened to Finnish social media in a long time." Star cleaner Auri is making some huge bank, even though she does the actual work for free—a turnover of hundreds of thousands of euros, MTV reported, stunned, in August 2022. In addition to numerous other Finnish and foreign media, the British public broadcasting network BBC also got excited about Auri in November 2022—so much so that they wanted to meet her, write several stories about her, and invite her to visit them. Maybe this is due to the fact that she has more than twelve million followers on social media.

That's an astronomical number; to put it in perspective, it is the population of our country (which is about 5.5 million at the moment) times two, and a little on top. There are always people who wonder if her videos are staged. Is Auri actually a money-hungry con artist? Or a nervous wreck making sure that nobody messes up her home? Can everything be fine when you are so frenzied about cleaning?

And then, when Auri once again cleans and arranges an unknown person's home and posts a video of it, an overwhelming amount of respect rains down on her. *What an altruistic gentle angel,* and *like God's gift to the world*—people sing her praises in the comment sections on TikTok and YouTube.

Auri's mother used to joke that reaching heaven for the whole family was guaranteed by Auri's work, even though her mother did not, and still doesn't, belong to the church. At the same time, as if half by accident, Auri has become the creator of a trend phenomenon of one of the least likely things possible: cleaning.

Most of us view cleaning with the grimness of an oncoming apocalypse, which is not free from sighs of annoyance, weeping, and even more weeping. For some of us, cleaning is the most stressful task; for others, it makes them fantasize about breaking up with a messy partner. Some may even second-guess their human worth when comparing themselves to their cleaner friend.

And then there is Auri. Auri, who makes dirt and mess sexy. She does not preach about losing control of life, nor does she mourn or pity the residents of these horror homes. But against all odds, she offers seemingly hopeless dumps her sincere love. On the sidelines, the residents of these homes get their share of it as well.

When I'm cleaning with Auri, I realize that the speculations on the forums aren't always off the mark. In essence, it is certainly not a burning desire to dust off other Mother Teresas, as anonymous commentators exclaim. It's not about saving previously unknown people from a total slippage in the wheels of society and, having succeeded, to polish her halo and let it weigh on her shoulders.

No, it is something else entirely. That is something else I now want to clear out from under the grime, and scrub to be recognizable to those who are interested. Just like Auri did on that floor, a memory ingrained in my cortex, at Oskar's place. And you should know in this book I won't do one of the key work phases of a cleaning gig: I don't polish at the end.

# CHAPTER 1

# WHO IS
# Auri Kananen?

## Born and Raised in Koikkari

If Auri's mother had held her in the womb for ten minutes longer, Auri's birth certificate would look a whole lot more interesting. But instead of staying in agonizing pain, she decided to push, and so was Auri Katariina born into this world at 9:20 a.m. on March 9, 1993. She was born in Tampere Central Hospital, from where her parents were soon discharged with their beautiful newborn.

They lived in a town called Koivistonkylä, which the locals call "Koikkari." It proudly stands in the southern part of Tampere, in between Nekala, Taatala, Vihioja, and Veisu. It's only a few kilometers away from the town center. Koikkari is like a textbook suburb, where children are playing in the sandbox, and the scent of barbecue hovers in the air. There's a school, a grocery store, a pizzeria, a gym, and not much more worth mentioning. Except maybe the fact that a world champion ice-hockey star, Raimo "Raipe" Helminen, was born and raised there.

Auri was the first-born child in her family, and when she was born, her mom was twenty-five and her dad was thirty-two. Her photo albums were filled with pictures of her lying on her back, and her side, and rolling on her stomach, like any typical child.

Neither of the parents had even thought about all of the things that could go wrong. What if Auri fell off a swing and hurt her head? What if she wouldn't make any friends? What if she became a bully? As parents, they weren't the type that would constantly worry about something bad happening to their child. They let everything roll at its own pace. This laidback attitude eventually influenced Auri's approach to life, too.

Even though little Auri was a new, weird addition to their lives, life with her seemed pretty carefree. Auri was an easy, happy child who would of course occasionally scream her lungs out, as babies tend to do. She would also soon get over her worries and continue her life as a happy, babbling baby. Auri was only three months old when she got to climb on the roof of their summer cottage, in the arms of her godfather, to install a TV antenna. None of the family members tended to coddle her. Even though Auri was also the first grandbaby of the family, she just fit right in, and it felt like she had always been a part of it.

Auri grew up to become a cheerful, energetic, and playful child. She didn't enjoy slow tinkering or monotonous games—she needed action. Decluttering or organizing, for example. When the new Harry Potter book came out, she had to get her hands on it instantly. Bratz were better than Barbies, and she also enjoyed taking care of her Tamagotchi. If you grew up in the early 2000s, you already know. When the beeping virtual pet died, it had to be brought back to life quickly. Even back then, Auri had determination and a feisty side.

When Auri gets mad, she's furious, but also tends to cool down quickly.

Auri's father remembers a particular ski trip to Levi like it was yesterday. Auri was only ten, and was about to head to the slopes for the first time. She just needed to get the ski lift in between her legs. The clock was ticking, and she just couldn't get the hang of it. At around five o'clock, it was time to head back to the cabin to make dinner, but Auri decided to try one more time. And that was the time she succeeded. After that, her father and the rest of the family could just dream about having dinner, since there was no way of getting Auri away from the mountains.

Auri was six years old when a new baby was born, her little brother Santeri. She was able to attend elementary school, just a stone's throw from home. But to do her time in middle school, she had to make her way to the city center. "To do her time" is not an exaggeration, even though it might sound like it. Auri was not interested in singing on stage at the spring ceremony or excelling in basketball; she also didn't care about being the class president, and the thing she least cared about was tediously studying for exam after exam.

In school, it was enough for Auri just to get through the classes. Sometimes she would peek at the answers of the person sitting next to her, since she hadn't studied for the exam herself. When her friends started attending house parties at the age of thirteen, Auri would tag along. She started applying concealer, and wearing tight tops and even tighter leggings, as all the other kids did. In her own words, Auri was an uncontrollable youngster; she had a mind of her own. She would skip school and run away from home to party. She would also occasionally smoke cigarettes, and get wasted. She was living a carefree teenage life, exactly the same as her mother had in her teenage years. It was clear that the daughter had inherited the party lifestyle from her mother.

After middle school, it was time to make decisions about the future, but Auri didn't have a clue what she wanted to do. So she followed in the footsteps of all her family members and applied to high school. There, she met her first love, who soon became her first boyfriend. They were together for many years.

When Auri turned eighteen, her parents got divorced, and her mother moved out. Since then, both her mother and father have found new partners. Auri understands her parents staying together so long because of their children. But even a child can sense a changed, chilling atmosphere around the house. For Auri, the divorce turned out to be a relief. Since then, both of her parents have been more open-minded and happier than they ever were in their years together. It also made Auri feel freer and happier.

After the divorce, Auri's father kept living in the family house, and still does to this day. A couple years after that, Auri broke up with her boyfriend and had to move somewhere else. She did own an apartment in downtown Koikkari, but didn't want to evict the tenant. Instead, she decided to ask her father for a place to stay—in the same home she'd once sworn she would never go back to. Auri's father offered her a room upstairs, and Auri took that offer. Living upstairs was peaceful, and their coexistence felt seamless. Whenever Auri came back home from wherever, she would shout out, "What's up, bunnies?" And he would mumble something back. After a while, Auri started dating again and moved out of her dad's. What her father misses the most is how clean she would keep their home.

Slamming doors, defying parents, using more swear words than other words in total, buying alcohol as a minor: that's not unheard-of for a teenager in Finland, and it applies to Auri too. But unlike other teenagers, Auri was depressed almost her entire youth. The first mental health issues rose to the surface at the age of ten.

The depression in her head planted in Auri the feeling that nothing made sense and, therefore, she didn't care about anything. The disease was present in many sections of her diary, which she wrote in computer files. There, it often states that she wanted to die, or was desperately looking for a way to survive.

"I have a feeling of not wanting to be alive. Everything hurts. Mentally and physically. Everything is black even if it isn't. I cannot find a single ray of light. Everything is behind a curtain, and it's impossible to breathe, or touch anything."

When you cannot understand, you cry, but you cannot even cry anymore. You're numb. You're paralyzed. You don't know what to be, what to do. Nothing changes. You don't want to move; you don't want to touch. You want to disappear. You want to die. You want anything to make the pain go away. You want to escape, but you're crippled by the pain. You have accepted the darkness. It doesn't matter if someone loves you, since it doesn't feel like anything.

"I wish I didn't wake up but always do."

No matter how hard she tried, she couldn't come up with a reason to stay alive. She wasn't even sure she would see her twenty-fifth birthday. And, since she would be soon dead anyways, or so she thought, she might as well make the most of what was left. It didn't matter whether she was chain-smoking, drinking booze, or hanging out in the streets with other kids. At some point, the group started to try drugs, which Auri also took part in, because why not. Even though she doesn't know any of those people personally anymore, she has heard that the drugs took the best out of some of them: "I do believe some of them have died because of those drugs. Many of them were broken and lost as well, and not all of them were able to get the help they needed."

By doing whatever illegal or stupid thing, Auri was able to awaken her sleeping feelings somewhat. When she disobeyed her mom or other adults, her seemingly meaningless life wasn't just swimming against the tide.

Then the excitement wore off again, and shifted into life-sucking emptiness.

Auri would also seek relief in harming herself, cutting her legs and arms, choosing places where other people couldn't see what she had done to herself. It was embarrassing and disgusting if someone noticed. Sometimes her friends would see the marks and ask her about them, but Auri was able to convince them that she had just accidentally scratched herself. One time, she had to be taken to the social and crisis services in the middle of the night. Blackout drunk, she was venting out her life to the police, who then made sure she would get the help she needed.

The writings in her diary took a turn to even worse: "I'm tired. Not scared. Dead tired. I wish I didn't wake up but always do. How long do I still have to live? I don't even want to think because everything is too much. It's too overwhelming. How do people manage through life? What am I doing wrong? When can I get out of here? How much is there left? It hurts, it hurts, it hurts. Then it doesn't hurt and then it hurts again. How many times does it hurt before it ends? Who is punishing me? I am sorry if I did something to deserve this. But I am suffering. How long?"

Then came the depression diagnosis from public healthcare at the age of fourteen. After waiting for six months, she started going to therapy. She had been able to access treatment early thanks to determined professionals. The youth psychiatric outpatient clinic did not swallow the claims that Auri initially made about not needing help. They did not believe that her behavior was nothing more than puberty.

Auri was never depressed in a stereotypical way that would have caused her to become apathetic and catatonic. In real life, very few tend to turn into ghosts of who they used to be—at least Auri didn't. She wouldn't remove herself from her friend group, or stop playing squash. On the outside, during her whole childhood, she was very outgoing and hung out with her friends at parties, or at least looked for one. When drunk, she would become even more chatty (and annoying, she says) until the alcohol started to wear off.

"Some people shop, some eat junk, but for me the most important way to escape was intoxicants. They helped me escape the emptiness. At the time my biggest reason to wake up was my morning cigarette. I can still remember how it felt taking a deep breath from a cigarette. For a little while I felt euphoric."

Healing from the depression took years. The biggest impact on her healing was therapy. It also helped when Auri met her first boyfriend, Eetu. The rebellious teenage years were fading away as adulthood came into the picture. At the same time, Auri moved out and started to take care of herself.

One day, after her recovery, Auri rode her bike in her childhood neighborhood in Koikkari. She couldn't remember if it was spring or summer, but the colors remained in her mind: They looked different than they had looked before. The brick walls, country roads, the trees lining the roads, the cars, and the birds were suddenly out from behind a foggy layer. Years later, they had color, light, and contrast again. Auri had to hit the brakes, jump off the bike, and take a moment. *What the frick, is this what the world looks like?*

Now it has been ten years since that bike ride. Auri has become a thirty-year-old world-renowned cleaner who smiles with all her teeth showing and laughs out loud. In her presence, there is some edge, like flickering sunlight that hurts the eyes if you have just woken up or are a bit sluggish. Auri has a habit of making a joke without much thought, and occasionally waving her hand to signal that it is not that serious. I'm sure she's always had the same detachment, but now there is no internal pain that makes her believe nothing matters.

When Auri recovered from depression, she learned to appreciate being healthy. She likes to cherish her health because she knows that if she isn't healthy, she cannot help others either. At least not by cleaning. After her tough teenage years, she realized that her boring routine-filled life suited her. In 2021, Auri revisited her psychologist. Auri had just become a full-time entrepreneur and gone viral. It was easy talking to this familiar face, because the psychologist knew everything from her past. Auri would no longer tell her how much she wanted to die because of her job. And what it felt like being a celebrity and reading nasty comments about herself. What would she do if the shit hit the fan and she was in the middle of a world-class fuss? They also talked about her fear of people not asking her to clean anymore.

Occasionally, when Auri cleans the homes of young people who have just passed their teenage years, her own past comes to haunt her—even when she is walking past a noisy group of kids in the streets. Even when she reads news about how a group of young people broke the windows of a convenience store, beat up an unsuspecting visitor, or something even worse.

"In those moments, I think that those kids must feel really, really terrible, and don't realize the horrible thing that they have done. If you do something stupid, there is usually a reason behind it. I feel empathy toward all teenagers, no matter what they are like. I did not either choose to be annoying or make anyone concerned about me. I didn't want to drink or smoke, but those were the

options I felt I had. I remember saying to my therapist that I just really wanted the adults around me to hug me, but I was too scared and too shut down to let them near me," Auri states.

After college, Auri also applied to volunteer for a crisis hotline in addition to her day job. There she answered calls from people in difficult situations. She listened with a keen ear, offering comfort and hope. Occasionally she met the people through the hotline face to face. If she weren't as busy as she is, she would still love to volunteer. Even though the stories were hard to hear, they didn't stay and haunt her. But they always made her feel as if she was doing something important.

"Someone might have told me how they had been raped and tortured as a child. That was obviously horrendous and made me realize that the world is a dangerous place. But when I put down the phone, I was okay. It didn't stay with me. I can't rescue anyone or undo what has happened, but what I can do is try to help," Auri says.

## Her Philosophy of Life

What is an indifferent person like?

If we go by the official definitions and general perception, it's a pretty reckless state. They show no care for anything. It doesn't matter to them.

The strange thing is that, although Auri is known as a selfless helper of others, she considers herself, first and foremost, indifferent. In a way, I understand what this is based on. I still prefer the term "detached" when talking about Auri. Auri is, first of all, a person who does not say no to even the wildest proposals. She might agree with almost anything and go along without prejudice, because in the end, everything passes. What does it matter if you lose face? Who cares if you go and choose by far the worst option? Things, no matter how earth-shattering they may seem at the moment, should not be given more power than they deserve.

> She can see a ray of sunshine
> even in the worst moments.

"Auri doesn't even really care about whether the end of the earth is coming or not, and she dares to say it out loud. That's probably what she means when she calls herself indifferent," says Anni, who is Auri's best friend. "Auri is also not interested in what other people have or what they own. Instead, she wants to hear what they think and feel and what they might want from the future."

Auri also sometimes thinks about death. She no longer hopes or believes that she will die in the near future, but death is still a natural, inevitable part of life, and a significant part of reality for her. She is not afraid to talk about death, or think that one day she will lie underground and turn to dust.

Auri's everyday life is embedded in a game of thought to which death is essentially connected. Sometimes, when she is driving, she asks herself if she would die content if she drifted into the oncoming lane and ended up lifeless on the side of the road. If she answers yes, she can continue her journey without a worry. But if she hesitates, something needs to be changed. To be happy in the present is everything for her after beating depression. You can never be sure if you'll wake up tomorrow.

Auri's philosophy of life is equally marked by the fact that nowadays she can see a ray of sunshine even in the worst moments, even if it sounds a bit corny. If the combination of school and work felt hard, she might have thought that, at least, she'd done the impossible possible by getting into school in the first place. If she finds herself stuck in traffic, she might think, *Damn, I live in a country where women are allowed to drive.* And that itself is something to be grateful for.

"I also have a certain detachment, so I don't panic if there are big changes to my plans. Whatever comes, comes, it doesn't matter to me. And when it's all the same, you can't get excited or fear the worst," Auri reflects.

"Challenges probably don't affect me, since I've been in that hell inside my head. Life is certainly not wonderful all the time, but nothing, not a single failure, is as terrible as the fact that you don't want to live," she continues. "If something goes wrong, so what? In any case, we are here for such a short period of time, which doesn't even weigh a gram in the scale of the universe."

"If I went to the gutter to do drugs, my friends and grandma would be quite sad, but then, on the other hand, it wouldn't matter at all. Once you release expectations and detach from outcomes, you can do anything. You can do the things that make you feel good. And if you happen to make a mistake, you can relax with the thought that everything passes."

## Auri's Cleaning Coronation

Every star often thinks about the moment that made them who they are today, or thinks back to the feeling that they have always known what they would become. The actress made her debut in the theater at the age of five, the policeman has been after the bullies since elementary school, and the surgeon used to practice operating on her Barbies.

Surely Auri danced around the kitchen with a mop as a toddler, sweeping the Bratz dolls out of her way? Well, Auri's parents don't necessarily agree with that. Instead, there were many times when Auri didn't exactly have the patience to clean her room. Auri thought that the self-made messes were too unimportant to tackle. One time, her room started to resemble a landfill. When her mom tried to get her to clean it, she acted like she couldn't hear her. That's when her mom had enough. She decided to put everything into garbage bags and carried them outside. "They'll stay there until you go get them yourself," her mom said, when Auri took a look outside.

It didn't take long until the mumbling girl went back and forth collecting her stuff from the yard. And soon the stuff found its place.

Auri's story does, however, have a sparkle of that Hollywood glamor. There were quite a few lists of chores that had to be taken care of before she was allowed to have her first phone, for example. The list included tasks such as washing the sauna, which, for nine-year-old Auri, was exciting. It was like night and day compared to cleaning her own room.

When Auri got out of elementary school on Fridays, she could visit a friend and clean their room. Auri loved to open her friends' drawers and organize the insides, since she could never be sure of what she would find. After a successful cleaning trip, the parents would give her money to buy herself some treats. With that money she would buy chips, chocolate, and sodas.

Auri's mother confirms the story. As a kid, Auri would indeed make her allowance by cleaning for everyone she knew. "I think she was pretty good at it," her mom says, "since she had a lot of houses to choose from. But cleaning at home was still unexciting for her, since the messes were self-made, and the money wasn't great either."

When Auri went to her grandmother's, she got to play a game which was played identically every single time. First, Auri put on her granny's finest dress, jewelry, high heels, and sometimes even a crown. Her grandmother was supposed to just lie down and pretend to be asleep. In the meantime, Auri threw clutter into the air and fluffed up some pillows and blankets. Then she would organize everything and put it back into place with her heels clacking. After a while, it was time for the grandma to wake up and be as grateful as she could be to the glamorous cleaning lady.

## Becoming the World's Best Cleaner

Auri probably wouldn't have started her career if she hadn't worked and studied to do it. Nor if she had been born in a different country. According to Auri, the cleaning industry is top-level in Finland. She believes that, in Finland, it is easier to get access to a lot of knowledge and supplies that the rest of the world can only dream about. Also, the quality of the supplies is from another world; for example, the squeegee: the love of Auri's life. In Auri's opinion, if you find a squeegee anywhere else in the world, it is not as high-quality and durable as in her home country. In Finland, the quality of cleaning supplies is superior to anything else that she has seen. When a Finnish cleaner uses a Taski, a floor cleaning machine, in Singapore there is someone using a Tasko. It's much more fragile than the original one.

Auri reveals that it isn't unusual in foreign countries to make cleaners clean a small spot for the whole day. Auri's mom has also come across cleaners who are only hired to clean toilets. The job doesn't require technique, but someone who will scrub, scrub, and scrub, and wake up the next day to come and scrub again. In Finland, it has also been necessary to develop the cleaning industry, since it costs so much more to hire someone in Finland

than it does somewhere else. It has not been possible to hire people to only clean the toilets.

Nor should we forget about the strict tradition of cleanliness in the country. The norm of cleanliness, which we carry with bittersweet pride, and which sometimes shoots us in the foot with its absoluteness. In the Nordic countries, people want to go to shopping centers that smell good, and walk around a city where overflowing garbage bags are not part of the streetscape. Our cleanliness is evidenced by studies that confirm the ingrained notion that hygiene matters. Cleaning professionals are taught exactly how quickly bacteria spread on public surfaces if they are not disinfected.

This is partly why cleaners in Finland are not looked down on. Auri has never had to be ashamed of her work, although over the years she has cleaned all kinds of places. Sometimes she, too, has been treated like she is invisible, but Auri has decided to respond to the behavior by scolding in an emphatically audible and cheerful voice.

Some cleaners also excuse their presence, apologizing more or less for having to interrupt more important activities by doing their jobs. They struggle with the stubborn notion that the work of a cleaner is not valuable and that it should be hidden. Auri remembers a colleague who had worked as a supervisor in another company, but then joined her mother's company as an ordinary cleaner. Returning to the cleaning, he was so embarrassed that he asked to be allowed to clean the fitness center late in the evening, when there would be no people there.

If Auri had gone public with a carefully considered agenda, it would have been a return of glory to the cleaners. Or rather, the creation of glory. Although cleaners are not discriminated against, based on Auri's experience, they have been visible at most in some corners. The cleaner is not considered a hero, but as soon as the cleaning is left undone, it will be noticed both on the soles of the shoes, and perhaps even as a musty stench in everyone's nose. Cleaning itself has not been trendy in the past, but rather viewed as mandatory. For centuries, the task was first assigned to mothers—or, in other cases, to the servants—inside the four walls, to an intimate and private space, which, however, also had social significance. "The home must be kept in order," the Marthas (a Finnish nonprofit organization) announced, to enlighten war-torn Finland and its citizens.

In this way, diseases would remain at bay and mortality would be eradicated. But if it didn't work out and chaos engulfed the home, then there was something wrong with the person (that is, the woman), unequivocally. Then, as the world modernized, cleaning didn't get that much attention. Rather, purity became an unwritten rule. Cleaning was easily overshadowed by decorating, gardening, and cooking. Instead of nice household chores, it was mandatory, and took time away from everything else. It's like a strenuously mundane brawl, and once you've started it, you dream of when it will be over. Rags and stinky buckets. Before Auri, not many people had been able, or even tried, to make cleaning look tolerable.

# CHAPTER 2

# CLEANING
## Philosophy

## Auri's Cleaning Love Book

**Q:** What's your favorite chore?

**A:** Cleaning the kitchen.

**Q:** What's the longest time you've spent cleaning up a single home?

**A:** Eighteen hours.

**Q:** In your opinion, what's the most unnecessary cleaning chore?

**A:** Stressing about cleaning up before you've even looked at your home properly.

**Q:** If you could take three pieces of cleaning equipment to a deserted island, they would be...

**A:** • Scraper, i.e., cleaning blade
  • PowerPaste
  • Microfiber towel

**Q:** What is the most difficult or tedious cleaning task?

**A:** For me, vacuuming.

Q: When cleaning, what do you listen to?

A: A crime podcast or a book in English. Sometimes also Spotify's Trending list, which doesn't take my focus away from cleaning.

Q: What's the worst misconception you want to correct about cleaning?

A: That cleaning is, and will basically always be, boring. The truth is that, if you give cleaning a chance, it can become a passion equal to your beloved hobby or favorite routine.

## What Distinguishes Me and Auri?

I sit at a work party where we can't stop celebrating the fact that summer is turning into autumn. We start playing a music-themed quiz game. I fill in the checkered paper with my educated guesses with a ballpoint pen. When the corner of the paper moves an inch, I realize what I have accomplished.

*Hell no*, I think, and there's a groan in the bottom of my stomach.

Have I destroyed my coworkers? No, but my boss's white kitchen table with my childish scratches? It certainly seems so. The blue streaks of ink don't go away, even if I rub them with a rag (Sorry for the wretched expression, Auri and other industry gurus, who I know hate the image created by the word *rag*).

Suddenly, the blood begins to hiss in my ears. I am one of those for whom the destruction of the property of others seems about the same as a mortal sin. I decide to text Auri in a panic. Tension tightens my digestive system in the same way as when you have sent a hot message to a crush and do not know how they will react to it. Auri sees the message almost immediately, thanks to the cleaning gods, and fiddles with her unequivocal answer for a couple of seconds. Auri advises looking for a cleaning stone, such as a Universal Stone, PowerPaste, or something similar.

"With a cleaning stone, it is gone as if by itself," Auri promises.

I run into the bathroom. As a result of the random opening of cabinets, I find what I am looking as if under the guidance of a higher power. There it is, a container that rests unsuspectingly at the bottom of a cupboard. I take it to the dining room like some rare gold bar. Then I start floating a damp microfiber towel on the surface of a white rock that turns sudsy. That's the way it goes now, I think.

It's really a go. After all that, the pen marks fade in a matter of seconds. They disappear as if they had never been there. Did I imagine the whole thing? Either way, I squeal, and others gather around me to marvel at my delight. I can't help but jump a couple of inches into the air. I would like to thank Auri for her generous efforts.

WELL FUUUCK

IT WORKS

THANK YOUUU

Seriously

Of course it works!

I'm ashamed to admit that I even doubted the functionality of Auri's trick, but I did.

In that moment, I realized what Auri's cleaning philosophy is all about.

*Auri secretly belongs to a camp of cleaning philosophers who shrug off dirt as just matter in the wrong place.*

When Auri sees something that people like me call an eternal dirt stain or an undigested mess, a cry of sorrow that raises blood pressure and can't be put off or organized on a better day, Auri's brain starts to tickle. Auri's brain starts to gather interesting thoughts:

*Ooo, I wonder if it would be nice to remove that dirt?*

Or:

*Wouldn't it be fun to clean up today a bit more thoroughly, or really quickly, or not at all?*

When Auri sees dirt or clutter at home, at a cleaning gig, or in public spaces, she doesn't know how to get frustrated or annoyed, no matter how hard she tries. Auri doesn't go through a routine train of thought in her head: *That, too, should be cleaned up. There's no way I could handle it, though, I wouldn't be able to. Wouldn't it be cool if all one's free time weren't spent cleaning?*

At that moment, if there is no time to address the dirt or mess that is lying in front of you, it is allowed to remain. You can remove it when you have time. And specifically remove it, not try to desperately get rid of it.

The attitude is liberating. I would argue that Auri secretly belongs to a camp of cleaning philosophers who shrug off dirt as just matter in the wrong place. For Auri, though, the dirt may not even be in the wrong place.

Rather, dirt is a lifeline. Like the dirt, the disorder—that is, the fact that the food packages have been scattered around the cabinet—does not make her fall into despair. This is probably due to a practical follow-up thought that often overwhelms Auri's mind. The thought is unsophisticated, yet decisive: *With what and how to remove the dirt or clutter?*

With what and how to remove the dirt or clutter?

Reflecting on the way dirt starts to disappear is even more epic than her first thoughts. Auri is excited about what she sees, because she knows she'll be able to eliminate it as soon

HAPPINESS CLEANING

as she takes action. Uncleanliness does not get a grip on her everyday life, nor does it crush her state of mind, because Auri controls it and not the other way around. She keeps dirt and clutter in the waiting room first. When she decides to put on her rubber gloves, dirt and mess can't do anything to her. Auri knows that you can tame any stubborn mess when you try enough tricks. The more dirt Auri encounters in her work, the quicker she can defeat it. Repetition makes her a cheerful professional. Who doesn't love doing something where they know they're unbeatable?

Auri believes that the joy many experience while baking a cake is the same joy cleaning brings her. Since Auri's flour thumb isn't at its peak, baking is an uncertain treat for her. The most important thing in baking is to measure the ingredients and follow the instructions closely (although neither of us is quite sure about this), but detailed recipes aren't always enough, if there's no instinct and the bakers can't lean on their knowledge. Inexperience makes the hustle and bustle clumsy, and you can't enjoy it. However, the more Auri bakes, learns some practical tricks, sticks her fingers in the dough, and messes up during the baking process, the more effortless baking becomes.

This also happens with cleaning. Even if you are not a cleaning guru at Auri's level, much of this attitude can be replicated in your own life as well. After all, your home can be cleaned, but sometimes it's not cleaned, simply because you don't have enough experience. Of course, things get easier when you have suitable, time- and effort-saving cleaning routines, and equipment, but more on that later.

## The ABCs of Falling in Love with Cleaning

There are people who focus on the big picture and are happy if their home looks clean from afar. Equally, there are people who do not know how to lower the bar on their standards. In a way, Auri is one of the latter group. If the timing is right, however, she too may strive for perfection.

When Auri visits someone's home, or a public space, her attention is not

drawn to the color scheme, surface materials, or décor. Instead, she focuses on details that reveal something about the kind of cleaning practices the place has adopted.

For example, once she saw an old piece of bubble gum pressed into the wall of the supermarket; they either didn't care or couldn't scrape it off. In a friend's toilet another time, the porcelain surface felt clammy, from which Auri could deduce that an acidic substance had splashed on the surface. instead of an alkaline one.

### CLEANING TIP

Acid never beats greasy dirt, but only eliminates odors and limescale. Also, if the drain basket in your sink is dirty, this is a sign that it has been scrubbed with a sponge instead of a dish brush, which, with its bristles, would fit into the tiny holes.

The difference between Auri and someone who gets anxious about dirt and clutter, like me, is that these things do not evoke negative feelings in Auri. Dirt does not disgust or irritate her. Especially, it does not make her ashamed, because a dirty or messy home is not the same as the person themself. Based on the level of cleanliness of the home, it is useless to draw conclusions about the superiority (or inferiority) of the resident. Especially when Auri is cleaning bomb-prone apartments, she rather plays with the dirt that has gotten stubborn. Even if the dirt has been hardening in the home for months, maybe even years, suddenly Auri comes as the professional she is, and it's all gone in no time. The feeling of victory is addictive, she admits.

One could say that dirt satisfies Auri as much as removing it. If it weren't for the dirt, there wouldn't be a victory in destroying it. Actually, Auri considers dirt her friend. A relatively close, but not best friend: you can't hate it, but you don't start sharing all the important things with it either, let alone swinging, and especially not getting married.

Seeing a guy, as well as dirt, is usually a joyful experience for Auri. Nevertheless, it is reassuring when a guy does not stay in your home. He is not a life partner with whom you need to share your everyday life, all your worries and weaknesses. Friendship is a more flexible relationship, where you can set boundaries more easily. Another difference from a spouse is that it's almost always fun with a friend, while with a spouse you sometimes have to go through difficult periods and deal with tricky questions. Do we share the same values? Do we still love each other? Will we be together for the rest of our lives?

Sooner or later, the guy, like the dirt, will ultimately return to his home. Of course, the timing of the visit is not always optimal. When a friend slams the door at the appointed time, you may feel exhausted or annoyed. Can you suggest to your friend that you see each other again when their batteries are charged? Or can your friend, especially someone a little closer to you, be left alone on the couch for a while, like Auri leaves her bestie Anni painting while she cleans? Auri thinks she can, and this also applies to dirt and clutter. It is also appropriate to say, "Let's take a look at it later, I'm not at my best right now."

Still, people tend to feel a sense of duty toward friends as well as cleaning. They stress themselves out if they have agreed to see someone, or have a cleaning day marked on the calendar. Although routines and prearranged things undeniably make everyday life more fluid, you should not feel so guilty that you hang on to them. Otherwise, they will begin to dominate you.

> Before you fall in love with cleaning,
> you have to start liking the dirt.

So before you fall in love with cleaning, you have to start liking the dirt. Dirt, dust, grime—whatever you want to call the guy. Right after, you have to accept the fact that you don't always have the energy. You don't always care or want to. Fortunately, the process continues a little more hopefully: You don't always have the energy, but soon the day will come again when cleaning, like seeing a friend, becomes more natural. Even better: You really start to miss it.

Since dirt must be regarded as a friend, its demonization must stop. It sounds quite toxic to have a friendship where you believe that the other person is more or less destroying the environment. There are very few homes where one would have to worry that a cluttered condition will damage the structures of the house and the health of the occupant.

"I go to filthy homes every week. That's why I also dare to say that nothing will happen even if you don't wipe the light switch for a year.

We are exposed to all kinds of grime all the time. As a child, we stuffed mud in our mouths, and nothing happened to us. The common areas are full of dust, and the bacterial content in a corner of a home that has not been cleaned is no match for a mobile phone that is in the palm of your hand all the time. Dirt is everywhere.

There are and will continue to be dirty places on this planet, and yet the world will not crumble. Perhaps some materials become brittle more easily, but that's really it. It's a bit like life moving forward, even though some stretches of road are in horrible condition and nobody ever drives on them. Everything in the world should be taken care of, but not everything is taken care of, and it doesn't have to be."

Before we can talk more deeply about the love of cleaning, Auri has to admit that just sharing cleaning tricks isn't enough. It is not necessarily the case that people who want to clean their homes strive for perfection in cleaning, or even that they have suitable cleaning supplies. Sometimes things stand in the way of the love for cleaning. Yes, even the goods that we need in our everyday life. Furniture, décor elements, loose objects, and straight-out junk. While dirt and clutter aren't Auri's blood enemies, the "stuff" might sometimes be.

The abundance of goods is by far the most common challenge for many households. Until Auri can reveal her unfailing cleaning tricks, she can't help but give her attention to the stuff—more specifically, to what skewed, even destructive, relationships many of us have developed with it. On the other hand, we cannot blame it solely on our own laziness or selfishness.

## Even the Keys Would Have to Be Thrown Away

I remember well the first time I met Auri for a newspaper interview. It was mid-January 2021, and the day was gray. The melted slush created its dams on the streets of Tampere and around its corners. I had arrived at Auri and Sami's home in Ylöjärvi, where we sat down at the table. Sami brewed coffee and Auri sipped tea from her half-liter water bottle. The table's surface was not filled with piles of papers or loose objects. I also noticed that the living room was not lined with decorative items that collect dust. The bedroom was equally understated with its unmade beds. The sight that awaited me on the ground floor of the apartment can be called obscenely unsophisticated: its largest room contained only cleaning supplies.

In the hallway of the apartment, two photographs of Auri and Sami hung above the closet. It's funny that, when talking about one's relationship with stuff, Auri highlighted the photographs and their meaning. She reflected on how we become attached to images, like they are living beings. What if all of Auri's photographs were transported into space?

*Everything that is most important is in the mind.*

For many, it would be considered an event of inconsolable crying and disaster, but for Auri it wouldn't. She refuses to become attached to objects, because she believes everything that is most important is in the mind. Memories do not disappear, even if the photos do.

Auri is equally saddened by gifts. She mentions the numerous woolen socks, knitted by Sami's grandma, that are sprawled in the closets of her home. Not a single pair was allowed to be donated or thrown away, for Grandma had made them with her own hands for Sami. Auri, on the other hand, neither wanted nor knew how to assign gifts received from loved ones to the top of the mountain of stuff.

"If I were someone's grandma, I'd probably like to knit for my grandchildren. I would also like it if the recipient of the gift did not take

on the gifts as a burden. Whenever I give someone a gift or a card, I say 'You can throw it away.' It is in no way disrespectful to me. No one will benefit if unnecessary junk is lying on the bottom of the cabinet unused. What's sadder is that the accumulating rubbish becomes a sea of junk that no one cares about."

It was easy for Auri to adopt a relaxed attitude toward stuff. After all, Auri's mother is even more liberal, a true world champion of saying goodbye to stuff and throwing junk into a garbage can.

Once, her mother found a pile of loose keys in a closet. She didn't think long before deciding to throw away the keys. It wasn't until a year after that happened that she realized that they had been

the spare keys to the apartments she had rented out. "But we got through it. In my childhood home, we were taught to not collect things unless they had an obvious purpose." Actually, Auri could well imagine herself throwing keys in the trash as well.

That's not to say Auri doesn't appreciate the stuff. She simply believes the ability to let go is the greatest appreciation of all. When things don't accumulate at home, Auri knows exactly where each item is.

> The ability to let go is the greatest appreciation of all.

According to Auri, the core problem with our relationship with things lies in the fact that people think they need something they don't. For example, some don't want to give up a working pen, even though their home is filled with usable pens, so much that they could never use them all, even if they live to be a hundred years old.

The most typical problem items are tiny loose objects, which alone do not cause harm. But when you start to accumulate a bunch of them at home, the situation is different. Little by little, a giant blob grows from a small one. Auri also adds gift items, trinkets collected from fairs, makeup jars, and electronics to her list of disgust. Cables are worst of all, for even those that have gotten into a knot we tend to spare for our lives, for safety, and let them fill the cabinets until they burst—even if the device that uses the cable in question has long since been replaced by a new machine.

In many cases, a main reason people store things is laziness—i.e., unwillingness to go through them dispassionately and sort them into items that can be stored, can be donated, or should be thrown out. The second reason is emotion: affection for stuff, the idea that the presence of goods brings security and meaning with it. This is the case, for example, with Grandma Auri. The times of shortage during the war are still etched in her memory, and from it springs the belief that nothing should be given up. You never know if there might be worse times ahead, when those things will come in handy. This can be seen especially at their cottage, where Grandma has accumulated piles of things, such as unused dishes.

Auri understands the idea well; there is some truth to it. Still, it's hard for her to identify with people who load intense emotions or unrealistic expectations onto stuff. Auri is not one of those who declares the drawings inherited from distant relatives to be sacred. When you don't forcibly create a story around an item, it doesn't get you wrapped around its finger.

At home, it is most important for Auri that there is room for the rhythm of cleaning up. If you don't have to wash load after load of laundry, it will feel easier to do it. You would never be able to wipe the floor if you had to clear the space first every time. As for her life, Auri sticks to one rule of thumb: you have to be able to pick things up with one hand, while the other hand cleans up. A time-consuming moving routine is not tempting, as it would eat away at even the motivation of a cleaning guru.

*Invest your time in what matters to you.*

So, while Auri is obviously something of a minimalist, her closet, for example, is allowed to look like an environment of destruction. The organized chaos feels cozy and not disturbing in the depths of the closet. The contents can be moved out onto the floor to search or, if you are in a hurry, you can grab the shirt you want, hanging between the others.

That is, there is no need to emulate the person who swears by sorting by patterns and colors if it does not fit you. Order will not bring you happiness if it is maintained for the sake of others, because you are afraid of receiving judgmental comments from those around you.

If something is disorganized but it doesn't bother you, you can let it be. You might leave it alone and say bye. Instead, invest your time in what matters to you.

## The Blessing of Generosity

The most common misconception associated with Auri in the public mind is that she is an incurable perfectionist. *She must clean up those dreadful homes because she does not tolerate dirtiness. Auri makes the dirt disappear so that all that remains is clinical cleanliness. Only then can Auri breathe easy.* However, when you spend one full day cleaning up with Auri, you realize how off-target that description is. Actually, Auri couldn't do even one cleaning gig if she were aiming for a flawless result. Striving for perfection would make the cleaning impossible.

The generosity that blesses cleaning gigs follows Auri everywhere. It gives cleaning a framework and moderation; it makes both starting and quitting easier. Auri's attitude is applied to all aspects of her life. For example, she does not thoroughly weigh through choices presented to her, but trusts her intuition and is not afraid of changing plans. If I had to choose one word to describe Auri, it would be uncomplicated. In other words, she does not deliberately make things more difficult.

So it's all about Auri's character traits. Some of us are striving for perfection in everything, and we are perhaps more exacting and patient than Auri. But with this attitude, it's more challenging to suddenly start taking a light-hearted approach to something. But could a home, with its dirt and mess, turn out to be the very place where you could relax a little? Because, if you loosen up a little, suddenly cleaning can become more fun. An energy-consuming, nerve-racking chore can turn into a hustle and bustle that elevates your state of mind. In Auri's (and her mother's) book, the uptight cleaner has a funny name: the pussyfoot. Auri has encountered them at work numerous times. A pussyfoot is a cleaner who gets stuck working on individual spots of dirt compulsively. They cannot break away from them until they are absolutely ready.

Auri's father, for example, has a thorough nature. While Auri was washing Dad's windows, he remarked how he would have liked to scrub the invisible holes where rainwater seeps in. Or, well, to be precise, he wouldn't have really wanted to do it. Dad just thought they *had* to be cleaned, which is why window cleaning had always felt like a chore and he never wanted to do it. When Auri grabbed the window-cleaning tools and got the glass free from smudges at a record pace, the work seemed too smooth in Dad's eyes.

If I had to choose one word to describe Auri, it would be uncomplicated.

If it turns out well, she will immerse himself in cleaning and forget about the passage of time. Cleaning can be enjoyable and rewarding, almost meditative. But it can also happen that cleaning turns into a constant source of stress, an impossible task. You don't want to start cleaning, because you know that it will take at least half a day. You can't stop in the middle of it. And even if the pussyfoot cleans their home for hours, they may feel afterwards that they have not accomplished anything. Cleaning which leaves one unsatisfied inspires few.

Along with the pussyfoot, there are those for whom cleaning means compulsory boredom. Either mercilessly boring or distasteful, perhaps disgusting. For them, cleaning brings to mind dirty, smelly rags and a nasty bucket, a never-ending labor camp from which glamor and peace of mind are far away.

However, most people are lukewarm about cleaning. They look at the vacuum with bored, sometimes glazed, eyes. For them, cleaning is an unwritten requirement, a norm that must be followed in order to belong, to dare to invite people to visit, and the reins seem to have remained in hand. They swear by quick cleaning, and look for ways to complete their cleaning chores with minimal effort.

Auri likes to challenge even those who say with bright eyes that they like cleaning. Do they really like the cleaning, or the end result of it? Do you need to like cleaning in the first place? Isn't it enough that the goal acts as a roaring engine of motivation?

You really don't have to get rid of it, let alone see cleaning as a big passion, if it doesn't shake your well-being or otherwise affect your life. But if cleaning up makes you feel in distress or burdened, Auri has aces up her sleeve.

She believes that both the pussyfoot and the indifferent can learn generosity, immaculate techniques, and the fact that there are many ways of doing things. One of the mainstay, universal tricks is to take inspiration from professional cleaners and talk about different sub-genres of cleaning instead of a single overall concept.

## Three Ways to Clean

To clean or not to clean: That is the question! If we are talking about cleaning, there are usually exactly two options: either cleaning or not cleaning. And if you clean up, then let's say you also polish your home from floor to ceiling. It is only after hours of sweating and swearing that you are free to crawl under the blanket and hum with satisfaction that you can live here again for a while. There is no problem with a weekly or monthly operation like that, per se. However, a person like Auri refuses to reduce her passion to such a modest, odorless and tasteless form.

Just think about running. Not many people can take the same jogging path monotonously, week after week and year after year. But when you change the route, get lost on side paths, or try to push yourself on steps and hilly terrain, the run immediately becomes somehow more tense. It takes on new shapes and shades. The basic movement, striding step by step, remains the same, yet not the same. There's also room to listen to your feelings. Sometimes you can last longer, sometimes you hit a wall in a quarter of an hour. Or, if the running metaphor doesn't resonate, think of any inexorably recurring thing: would you like to eat the same casserole week after week, or listen to the exact

same song over and over without the possibility of changing the playlist?

Those who clean professionally have to approach cleaning as a constant front of change. They cannot choose their cleaning method based on how they feel that day, but they adapt to wishes and the promised reward. Some sites need a sparkling result, others settle for a rougher aftermath, in which case it is enough to clean the most significant dirt and the most obvious stains out of sight. A cleaner cannot become attached to a tried and tested way of cleaning, but must approach each gig within the framework given to it.

There are actually three different ways of cleaning in cleaner language: checkup cleaning, maintenance cleaning, and weekly cleaning. Adopting these categories for cleaning your home may be appropriate, especially if cleaning is not a meaningful and natural part of everyday life. Auri also makes use of different cleaning styles in her life, jubilantly messing around.

She doesn't swear by major cleaning, primarily because her home never gets to a condition where it's necessary. In order to keep her love of cleaning strong, for Auri it's not a matter of hours, but a hobby that can accommodate all kinds of things. Both in-depth sessions and quirky, one-off tasks are handled just as willingly.

First Auri wants to highlight the checkup. As the name implies, you first take a look at the home to see in what condition it is. Let's scan around the apartment, and only then think about the game moves. Sometimes checkup cleaning can mean washing dishes, piling books back on the shelf, cleaning stains from the kitchen table, and wiping crumbs that have fallen to the floor. It saves time and does not take too much of a toll. However, the checkup requires stopping. It cannot be done by engaging in familiar activities out of habit. Instead, we have to think: what should we or should we not do here? Those who clean up quickly will notice that it may not be necessary to constantly polish the table.

Maintenance cleaning, on the other hand, is routine and mechanical work. Sometimes that's fine too. It does not require the cleaner to go through the home in advance. Maintenance cleaning is done as always.

It is typical, for example, that the floor is wiped, the trash is taken out, and the sink and tap are wiped to a shine with a cloth and detergent.

By cleaning up in a sustainable way, you can turn your brain offline and please the parts of yourself that purr with pleasure when things are done as they always are. Auri doesn't admit to being a loyal maintenance cleaner, but she is aware of why people prefer it. You simply don't always have the energy or the desire to spend your time checking whether it is appropriate to pay attention to the dust bunnies on top of the cabinet instead of cleaning the sink.

Thirdly, Auri talks about weekly cleaning. In this case, the cleaner must thoroughly inspect the home. From top to bottom, from side to side, from room to room. Despite its name, weekly cleaning can be done, for example, once a month. Instead of forcing yourself into age-old chores, you can also focus on surprising points at home. Where has dust accumulated like the most? Does a wardrobe or spice drawer need rearrangement? Could we finally take those winter clothes that were lying in the hallway to storage? When it comes to weekly cleaning, you are allowed to enjoy yourself a little and let the clock tick. During the weekly cleaning, you have time to be creative. Try a new detergent or technique to see if it works better than your traditional method.

Tried and tested routines can also be tweaked or alternated with each other. That's how Auri works, for example, when cleaning the toilet. Each week, she alternates between cleaning bathroom surfaces with an acidic substance and with an alkaline substance, such as dishwashing liquid.

An acidic substance with a pH value of less than seven and an alkaline one with a pH value of more than seven remove various kinds of dirt: acidic for limescale, alkaline for greasy dirt.

In addition to creativity, a happy cleaner is asked for mercy. Although Auri is not allergic to the scheduled cleaning days familiar in many families, she does not feel that it is the only right way to keep the home in order.

Some people don't book a Saturday on the calendar for a three-hour, well-timed cleaning marathon, but instead clean a little frequently, so the home doesn't even get too messy. Then keeping cleaning days, with stuck formulas and rules, just out of habit is a waste of time.

Instead of a routine, could you focus on one special task, such as cleaning the oven, arranging the wardrobe, washing the sofa covers, or wiping the dust from the walls and ceiling? To fix your eyes on chores that are usually left behind because of vacuuming and cleaning the pool?

On the other hand, Auri wants to give equal weight to mandatory household chores. They may not be cleaning in the truest sense of the word, but they are time-consuming nonetheless. Auri also encourages you to include hanging laundry and taking out trash as part of a happy cleaner's large playground. If you return to the language of the cleaner for a moment, Auri says that she combines checkup and weekly cleanings in her home. Instead of clinging to routine and always cleaning her home in the same way, she relies on her senses. If the floor has not gotten dirty during the week, there is no need to give it attention. Although it takes a while to go through the home, Auri believes it pays off. When you don't get stuck in an age-old routine, you can do what is necessary at any given moment. It is useless to drag a rattling vacuum to every corner of the apartment when there are no crumbs or dirt to be seen.

The example is apt, as Auri almost never vacuums. It's a waste of time for her, and takes time away from more rewarding cleaning chores, although everyone is allowed to manage their home in a way that suits them (the main thing is that cleaning doesn't feel too burdensome). Through her profession and the cleaning gigs she has done, Auri has considered something often: What facts and quirks could make cleaning fun?

The obvious thing is that cleaning isn't just philosophy and stuffing your former bad attitude into the shredder. It's not about taking an ego-based action, implementing a New Year's resolution, focusing on what you learned from yoga, or unleashing tearful rage into dirt. In all its mundaneness, cleaning is more about grabbing a cloth (not a rag, certainly not a rag, and never a rag, as, in Auri's opinion, it is the most disgusting word in existence!) and sticking your hands into dirt and mess.

Despite being mundane, cleaning doesn't have to be strenuous, and especially not sickening.

It doesn't have to be a chore that serves as a means of punishment in a family with children, or sows endless strife between lovers. Instead, it could be something you might enjoy. Something that can be approached with fire. That's just the way it is: there's no need to hate cleaning. Instead, it's something adults can truly learn to love.

# CHAPTER 3

# WHEN

*Auri*

# CAME,
# CLEANED,
# AND

*Conquered*

## The Beginning of Cleaning with an Audience

Everything begins with cleaning a stove. The exact day is July 27, 2020. Auri posts a short video clip of her removing hard stains from an old stove. Her cousin's girlfriend has just moved to a new apartment, and the previous tenant left the stove in an unholy state. The frustrated girlfriend asked for Auri's help, since she knows what a good cleaner she is.

She is so excited about the task ahead that she decides to film it. In the background, she adds some techno beat that reminds her of the nightclub. The way the video was filmed is a bit clumsy, considering the way she films these days. The image sways a bit,

but the finished product can be seen clearly. The blackened stove is now sparkling clean.

Before posting the stove video, Auri had been sharing her cleaning videos with her friends. They would testify to her scrubbing the dirty crevices of her home with a toothpick while bursting with joy. Her friends would often tell her to share her tips with the world.

It has to be said that, at that time, Auri was even lazier about using social media than the average Finn. On Instagram she had three hundred followers, and she knew each and every one of them. She didn't post that often about her meals, trips abroad,

or squash practice. At that time there weren't many cleaning videos out there, other than a few crazy Americans emptying a few detergent bottles into the toilet.

It was the first summer during Covid. Auri was working in her mom's company, and they were in the middle of hiring for the summer. Auri had noticed that there weren't enough applications in their inbox. The kids didn't want to clean; instead they chose basically any other job they could get even if it meant they had to work on half the salary and have worse hours. Could her cleaning videos change even one young mind about cleaning? That's one thing she thought about before posting her first video.

The video got three hundred views, and a comment from someone that Auri didn't know. Auri thought that was amazing, and it got her to make more videos. At least there were some people who liked her content. Next she filmed a video of cleaning a couch and some dirty sneakers. Her loyal viewers also found those videos, but they didn't become viral hits. A video of Auri cleaning the interior of a car did, however, get hundreds of thousands of views overseas.

The summer went on, and Auri kept filming as much as she could, after work and other duties. Coincidentally, she ran into her ex-boyfriend at the gym. During the workout, the ex mentioned spiders that had made a nest on his balcony. He asked if Auri wanted to come and clean his apartment. Auri instantly said yes. She was glad to clean an apartment that she herself had spent some nights in a few years back.

That video went far and ignited vigorous discussion. When Auri posted it, even viewers from the United States said what a pushover she was for cleaning an ex-boyfriend's apartment. Who would be so in love with someone as to clean his apartment even though he has a new girlfriend? She should "stop being a doormat and grow herself some balls," some commenters said. At the time, nobody knew the person behind these videos. When the current girlfriend found out about Auri's little visit, she was also a bit shocked and hurt. The world clearly didn't understand the fact that, for Auri, it wasn't about her love for her ex, but her love of cleaning.

Instead, there was love in the air somewhere else.

## A Date of Faith

That summer had been suffocatingly hot. Auri had worked her butt off, worked out, and filmed herself cleaning. She had also spent some time on Tinder, but not looking for anything serious, maybe just looking out of boredom. She would open the dating app when she had nothing else to do and would religiously swipe left. Left, left, hmm, left. Right? Right!

One right swipe seemed to be nice and had potential. It would also be his birthday soon! He was turning thirty. Even though Auri wasn't looking for anything serious, something about this man had sparked her interest, so they exchanged numbers. On his birthday, a gift package icon would appear after his name on Snapchat. If she pressed that, the app would send a greeting notification to him. Auri didn't settle for a simple greeting; instead, she offered him a free home cleaning.

> You don't have to be home for the whole time I'm doing my thing. Because it could take a long time! So you could maybe go out and play golf or whatever you want to do.

> Of course you can stay home, but I'm not that great company during that.

That's what Auri wrote to him and added a smiley face.

The man was stunned (who wouldn't be?), but gladly took her offer. But he indeed wanted to stay home to keep her company. He also gave her permission to film the cleaning as long as he stayed anonymous. Then he sent pictures of his place at Auri's request.

> I don't want you to spend the whole of Saturday night here, so I won't make any more mess.

> At least don't clean anything before that! I'm so excited.

The conversation went on the next day, when the man asked her when she was coming over.

> Is it alright if I come at 1 p.m.?

> Fine by me. I have to be in Pirkkala at five for a grad party. I have no idea how long you're going to clean, but I'm sure it won't be that long.

> Well, in that case, I could come a little earlier! So what time can I come over?

> Anytime is fine.

He couldn't have understood what he had agreed to and what kind of a cleaning maniac was typing on the other side of the screen.

At ten o'clock on a Sunday morning, Auri rang his doorbell. When he answered the door, Auri was stunned, since the sight was even worse than it looked in the pictures. And no, it wasn't about the guy. He looked pretty much as he should have, and even his personality matched his profile. It was about the apartment—the surfaces were almost shining, and everything was in its place. Auri thought that there might not be anything to clean until she took a closer look. She climbed onto the kitchen counters and took a look at the top of the cabinets. A smile came to her face when she saw the dust.

Soon she noticed other spots the guy had not given much love on his cleaning days. The top of the toilet was blackened by dust, and the sink also had some dirt in it. The stove hood was covered in grease, but the kitchen sink was spotless. Luckily, the oven looked like it had been hit by a nuclear explosion. When Auri started cleaning, the guy stood by and watched her go. Soon he wanted to join in the cleaning, and not too long after that, they were both elbow-deep in detergent. After a few hours, he went to get some food from Pancho Villa. He persuaded Auri to take a quick lunch break, and then they headed back to tackle the dust and grime.

This man was Samuel, who Auri then called by his real name, Sami. That Sunday, Sami knew that the proposition for the free cleaning was actually true. He had watched Auri open and wash the floor drains for hours. She also found some toothpaste stains that had dripped off of Sami's toothbrush. Auri had been cleaning from nine to five, and would have continued if Sami didn't have to leave to attend the party.

Since the cleaning wasn't done, they set up another date, for the following Sunday. Sami, that mysterious dirty guy, had wooed Auri, who would have loved staying single for a while longer. At that time, Auri was reserved when meeting new people, and she definitely would not date them. But Auri and Sami's quirky first-time meeting led to some not-that-quirky following meetings.

In addition to getting a life partner, Auri also got her first viral video by cleaning Sami's apartment. It was something she was not expecting, and it also got the wheels rolling. In other words, she posted a video in which she openly said she had met an interesting guy online and they had arranged a date. In the background, there was romantic music playing, and it jokingly shows how Auri asked his permission to film the act. The viewer was stunned when, instead of filming "the deed," she filmed wiping the dust off his cupboards.

The video got five million views on the first day, and instantly made Auri into a viral hit.

◇ ◇ ◇

Auri published the video on September 6, 2020, and had 20,000 followers. The next day there were over 100,000 followers. The video was viewed all around the world, and people were making noise in the comment section. Even though Auri thought the home was too clean to begin with, Sami was soon labeled a pig who was living in mess and filth and not taking care of himself. Nowadays the video has over twenty million views, so it's still one of her most-viewed videos.

Cleaning Sami's home also gave Auri her first spot in the headlines of magazines. One tabloid called her and wanted to know what kind of person was behind these videos, and how she was dealing with the fame. Auri told them everything they wanted to know, but she didn't think anyone would care. She was certain that they weren't even going to publish the interview, since she is not that interesting.

It didn't take long for that thought to be proven wrong. She felt weird, as if her face didn't belong on magazine covers. But she did get used to the fame quickly. After the first article, it didn't feel weird anymore, no matter where her face ended up. Life had changed and there was no going back, but that didn't scare her. She didn't want to speculate, since you never know what will happen. It might be just a one-time thing and the fame would fade as quickly as it blew up. It would be wiser to just concentrate on what was important: cleaning. She had only scrubbed a few places, and the dirt wasn't going to run out.

# Reaching Millions

Being a star cleaner doesn't call for a glamorous life and sharing every detail of it. Auri doesn't feel like a part of the influencer club, who work their butts off to stay on top, she says, meaning those who film themselves bare-faced, going about their day, sharing everything they eat or drink, what they buy, or the plastic surgeries they get. Auri is followed for her cleaning advice, not for her face or fashion sense. That's also why she doesn't really have insecurities about her looks or worry about life becoming boring, and so her videos are simple. Auri doesn't think her views would drop even if she changed her signature pink apron or quit applying makeup altogether.

Even still, filming cleaning videos involves a lot more than just taking a cloth and adding a little detergent. It requires heavy-duty equipment, for example. When things started to take off, Auri decided to get herself better equipment. Before this, she had just filmed with her phone in her hand, and she didn't have any lights or camera stands.

Although the filming equipment was updated, her vision still remained the same: find the dirt and destroy it. In other words, Auri was focusing solely on individual problem areas. It would have been a natural path, as Auri saw and still sees dirt everywhere. Dirt does not disgust or irritate her, but her eyes stick to it. If Auri is on her way to the store, for example, it is not unusual for her to notice a smoothie spill on the floor. On a whim, she can turn on her heel, pick up cleaning equipment from the car, come back, and start cleaning Koskikeskus (a shopping mall in her hometown, Tampere) in a squatting position. Those passing by might stare a little, but it's probably not the weirdest thing to see.

In addition to public places, Auri planned to record cleaning her own nooks and crannies, and sometimes friends' homes, in her videos. Yes, you read that right, just friends' homes. In other words, no apartments that have been dirt-bombed by previously unknown people. This is how it all started. But coincidences lead to other things, and the future certainly cannot be predicted, as the case of Auri shows.

On the fifth day of October 2020, a woman from Tampere sent her a message. She went straight to the point and asked Auri for cleaning help. The woman's husband had recently hanged himself above the staircase, and she had been left alone with three children. The message was accompanied by pictures that revealed that the home had become almost uninhabitable.

Something was moving inside of Auri. It was not disgust, frustration, or pity for the woman. It was a strong feeling that said, *I am meant to do this.*

That Friday, autumn was already so far advanced that leaves were falling from the trees at a steady pace. The streets smelled of mud and wet asphalt. The taverns were empty due to the coronavirus, so those who had been busy during the workweek recharged their batteries by running at the track, or maybe lying on their couch at home. Auri, on the other hand, gathered up her cleaning supplies at the end of the working day and drove to the previously unknown woman's house. The woman was at the door waiting for her. She gave Auri brief instructions, and then left with her children to get out of the cleaner's way. There Auri stood, alone in a strange, mess-filled apartment.

"What on earth, Auri?" her friends and mom asked her in messages, when Auri revealed her whereabouts to them.

"Dippa-dappa-duu, what's this, cleaning up," Auri thought, trying to convince herself that there was nothing weird in the activity. Afterwards, Auri herself was amazed at what she had gotten herself into.

Cleaning, both physically and mentally, turned out to be much tougher than Auri had imagined. Somewhere in the middle of it, she began to feel faint. She actually had to run to the bathroom to be sick, because her insides were twisted around by it. As the evening turned into night, fatigue made her eyes water. Although Auri was supposed to return home for the night to sleep, she accidentally fell asleep on the couch in the apartment. The good thing was that it was easy to continue the work from the couch as soon as she woke up the next morning.

The next day, the home began to shine again. It seemed like a bit of a miracle to Auri. When the family got home, the mother burst into tears with a mixture of relief and gratitude. The children, too, rushed to hug Auri, who had done magic to the house.

It was Auri's first cleaning gig at a stranger's house. When she returned home, she felt like she could sleep for a day straight. At the same time, she felt like it was impossible for her to even stand still. The video captured from the gig was soon available for everyone to see. It garnered an astounding twenty-three million views on TikTok. The video certainly appealed to viewers with its lack of sophistication. No one had seen anything like it before. Does someone really go and clean up a stranger's homes out of the goodness of their heart, without asking for compensation?

A month passed, and Auri was able to clean for a stranger for the second time, this time at the home of a man with schizophrenia. She had never seen a dirtier place in her life. It was so dirty that when she saw it, Auri forgot to breathe for a while. Not out of shock, but out of joy that was spilling over. The feeling was also passed on to others, as the video was viewed millions and millions of times. After a couple of days, Auri crossed the milestone of one million TikTok followers. It was night, but Auri tried to keep an eye on it to see the number turn into seven digits. At 1:30, her eyes were closed, and in the morning, Auri woke up as a cleaner with a million followers. After that, the follower count slowly lost its meaning, a bit like what had happened with the first newspaper article.

## The Cleaner from Finland

Avalanche, domino effect, inexorable chain reaction. That's what it looked like to an outsider, and that's how it went. Suddenly, Auri was being talked about on all continents. A German television channel was the first to fly its journalists to make a documentary about Auri. Followers also began sending her screenshots of media in their own country, where Auri was being praised in different languages, sometimes in Thai, sometimes in Hebrew. British tabloids wanted their share, too, of a strange, cleaning-loving Finn. Auri agreed and agreed to all interview requests, including *Yankee* magazine and an Espoo-based housing company magazine. The more places she appeared in, the more dirt-bombed homes she could reach, was her thinking. The bomb homes, as Auri calls the targets of cleaning gigs, are the only sites that pose a genuine challenge to her—the places that make the heart flutter every time, right at the first encounter at the door, and even after the apartment is cleaned and it's time to close the door behind her.

Auri's father, who also works as a sales director, soon noticed how customers abroad reacted when they heard his last name. "Are you related to Auri Kananen, the cleaner?" The father nodded in confusion and confirmed the suspicion as true. "Yes, she is my daughter, actually."

*Seiska*, a Finnish tabloid, is probably the only one of all the media in the world to whom Auri refuses to give an interview. When the gossip magazine calls at regular intervals, she replies the same way every time: "Grandma has told me not to, so I have to be quiet." Grandma hasn't really told her that, but Auri just doesn't care to give *Seiska* comments that would certainly be misrepresented, or at least put in a questionable light. They come up with headlines about her regardless, so they don't need to support what the subject of the story herself says, Auri has reasoned.

In 2020, Auri was invited to join the US-based *Good Morning America* program remotely. She was told the task would be to ask the presenters questions about cleaning, in the spirit of Christmas. After a couple of phone calls, she didn't hear from the show's creators for more than a month. Auri thought they had forgotten the whole thing.

The night before the live broadcast, she received an email with a script and immediately afterwards a message that the performance would be postponed. Soon her inbox was pinging, and the cancellation was canceled. After all that, Auri was to be on the line the next day, three hours before the show. And so she was. While waiting, she was able to hear in real time how the broadcasters were messing around. The long dress rehearsal went pretty much off a cliff. The connection was broken, and Auri couldn't get the English words out of her mouth as she should have. Her speech was muddled, and the stressful situation was not improved by not being able to read from the script.

In the end, Auri negotiated permission for herself to have cardboard question tags for the show. Half an hour before the broadcast, she listened to the printer slowly juggling and spitting paper into the air. After that, she taped the papers to cardboard to use as notes.

*What is this life of mine?* Auri thought, not knowing whether to cry or laugh. There was panic in the air and her stomach was aching, even though she is almost never tense. "That video connection went awry just ten minutes before it was supposed to turn on," she recounts. "I couldn't hear or see them until someone texted me and told me to close the line and go back. I had three minutes at that point. Miraculously, I was able to make the connection work. I just heard them when they counted that ten, nine, eight, seven... Then I thought that this would be the best day of my life, as long as I didn't participate and embarrass myself—I would be annoyed if that happened. I just started asking the three questions I was supposed to ask. When that broadcast finally ended, I shut down the machine and cried for a long time. I still haven't been able to watch that show," Auri recalls of her ordeal.

However, despite her feelings about it, the broadcast is seen as a fun, relaxed, iconic moment for Finland and its people, who are always so excited when a Finn gets into the international spotlight.

Auri's English has largely improved under pressure. The language was used in interviews, sponsorship meetings, and videos. It is demanded a lot, but it was precisely because of her English that Auri almost didn't graduate at one point. If the inspectors grading the exam with a magnifying glass had taken even one more point away, she would have failed.

Because of all the publicity, Auri eventually hired an English teacher. It paid off. When Auri cleans up, she also always listens to podcasts or books in English, so that she can learn to be a perfectly fluent world citizen who changes languages on the fly.

# Farewell, Day Job

Before Auri fully transitioned to being a full-time cleaning diva, her candle burned from both ends, or at least that's what it looked like in the eyes of those around her. Auri would first work a full shift at her day job, and then continue with a cleaning gig, editing videos, and going through her email. The hours of the day ran out all the time, so Auri cheekily stole them from her night's sleep and from the free time she would usually spend seeing friends.

Finally, in March 2021, Auri finally had to tell her mother that she would leave her supervisor duties at her mother's cleaning company and focus on making videos. Once they found her successor, Auri registered her limited liability company and became a full-time entrepreneur. It had never really crossed her mind before, but once the paperwork was in order, Auri soon adapted to her new everyday life. In one big swoop, she took over all social media channels, including YouTube. In desperation, with the support of her friends, she translated sentences into English and kept her fingers crossed that the facts would even be passed on. Finally, she hired an editor, Nea, who at the same time became her translator.

Auri still handles everything else work-related on her own, although, to be honest, further help would be in order. It's partly because of the loneliness, partly because she agrees to everything—the calendar is always crammed, it is hard to deny it. Even though her day job is in the past, Auri still doesn't have much time to see her friends or visit places she used to. Her best friend, Anni, is an exception. Like Auri, she has risen to international fame by running the Hydraulic Press Channel with her husband. In their channel, they film their hydraulic press crushing a variety of strong items, which, like Auri's cleaning, is strangely satisfying to watch. Anni and Auri's friendship is reminiscent of a childhood friendship, where they chat for hours and share all their secrets.

Anni understands the laws of Auri's current work, and sometimes their time together is when Anni draws, paints, or makes sticker books, and Auri cleans or edits a video. The friendship that started with one harmless LinkedIn post took off with a bang. In a couple of months, it had turned into a friendship, where every morning begins with an exchange of messages. For Anni, Auri is a family member, a favorite person with whom you have to stick together for the rest of your life.

As a result of the publicity, Auri has visited numerous galas and media events. But Auri hasn't agreed to stay mute in the big world's gigs. Grandma, who is one of the most important people in Auri's life, has said that Auri has left Koikkari to conquer America, and that's exactly how it's gone. Auri is still happiest in one environment: hands in dirt and in grimy homes.

However, publicity is publicity, no matter what you do. That is what Auri has noticed. In Finland, Auri has fallen into the claws of *Seiska*, which she has tried to avoid by all means, as have many other stars. The gossip magazine has reposted, for example, about a cleaning gig done by Auri, after which the housing company's garbage dumpster was full of garbage bags:

*HUGE MOUNTAIN OF GARBAGE! DID AURI KANANEN, A SOCIAL MEDIA CLEANER FOLLOWED BY MILLIONS, LEAVE BEHIND THIS PILE OF JUNK? STARK IMAGES.*

HAPPINESS CLEANING

And then, to stir up the pot, the magazine continued:

*THE SOCIAL MEDIA CLEANER FOLLOWED BY MILLIONS LEFT BEHIND
A HORRIBLE PILE OF JUNK—NOW AURI KANANEN INTERVENES
IN THE FUSS AND OFFERS THE ANSWER: "I DON'T MIND."*

Another time, *Seiska* did a story about Auri opening up on her
Instagram about the woman who bailed on her:

*THE MEASURE OF THE SOCIAL MEDIA CLEANER FOLLOWED BY MILLIONS
WAS MET: AURI KANANEN ACCOUNTS FOR A DEPRESSED WOMAN
STANDING HER UP: "IT WAS DEEP."*

At first the headlines made her laugh, but then Auri got serious. "You know, I've been thinking of not doing public work for more than maybe just a couple of years. Then I will shut down social media completely and start doing something else. Even though I enjoy being in the public eye, it also scares me, especially because even a small mistake can wreck everything.

"I don't think I'll ever fall for some bad mistake that people and the media are eager to get caught up in. I can't know what that mistake is, but it's coming, I'm sure of that. Not everyone was created to endure the bravado that celebrities face. Most want to live their own lives, where, at most, only your loved ones know about your mistakes. Despite all the possible downsides, I feel that I am doing well with publicity so far.

"Without it, I wouldn't have a chance of finding bomb houses to clean up. That's the most significant reason why I want so much visibility and agree to all kinds of interviews and programs."

### ABOUT GETTING RICH

Auri's childhood was by no means poor. It didn't involve hunting for discount items or meticulously checking the account balance before payday. Their house was big, the family was able to go on holiday trips to somewhere warm once or twice a year, and Auri and Santeri were free to do what they liked. Despite this privilege, both were taught to earn their own money from a young age.

When it comes to the financial success she has achieved through her platform, Auri speaks with bewildering frankness atypical for a Finn. Her main source of income is various YouTube ads and sponsors like Scrub Daddy and Sinituote, who pay Auri a kind of monthly salary. Neither of the sponsors influence Auri's work by dictating conditions for what she does, such as what kind of apartments Auri should clean or what the videos should say.

Auri speaks frankly about all this, and the words are light-years away from the cloud castles. I know that Auri's life is almost the same as it was before the explosion of popularity, if the work schedule is taken out of the equation. She doesn't buy designer bags or ego-boosting sports cars or plan to build a palace somewhere. She buys the same groceries as before, goes to the same gym, and spends the most money, well, probably on food. Flying first-class to faraway countries doesn't make her soul hum, either. What matters is what to expect at the destination. If the goal is an unknown person's dirty home, there may well be a lot of hype in the air. But the older she gets, the more Auri finds herself resembling her grandma on holiday trips, for example. "Ho ho, enough is enough, let's go home," both Grandma and Auri tend to sigh, in their last few days lingering in the warmth of the south, or in the lovely alleys of a city resort. Home is always the best, though.

If she doesn't want to boost her life with money, what does Auri want from money?

"Freedom," she replies in a flash, and I shouldn't be surprised by the answer anymore.

Freedom means she can continue doing what she loves and making people's lives better. It means having enough so that she can focus only on what her mission is. Freedom means that, when parking a car, you don't have to think about how much it will cost to park. It is also the case that, if you need to get your hands on a product right now, you can easily order it immediately without thinking about the price and not searching in stores for unbeatable offers. And, above all, freedom is a way of continuing doing what Auri loves and helping people for free.

"When I was in therapy and was fourteen years old, I had to think about what would help me. I wondered if I could get all the money in the world, would that help? And then I was like, you know, it wouldn't help. Money still doesn't bring me happiness, but it brings, above all, freedom," Auri says.

# CHAPTER 4

# AT THE
# CLEANING

*Gig*

## Auri's Process

### *No Gig Without a Picture*

Yet another cry for help is in the inbox. It is the summer of 2022. Someone has shared their story and is hoping that Auri will arrive at their home. If a video takes off or Auri gives an interview, the email app may beep hilariously often. When it comes to contacting those in need, she always first binge-reads all the messages she receives.

Other contacts, whether they are overwhelming job offers or gossip, are overshadowed by requests for help. On our first day of cleaning together, there were eleven contacts by noon, all from abroad. The number is gratifyingly high. The kind of luck that would bring a dozen messages from Finland a day, Auri has not yet encountered as of this writing. However, the rarest are the weeks when no one sends a message.

At the same time, as we eat our lunch salads on the terrace under the scorching sun, Auri scrolls through her email with a curious and expectant look on her face.

"Maybe not, it's a really cool home," she mumbles at one, and shows me some pictures. It's true, the apartment is not nearly as messy as Auri's properties in general.

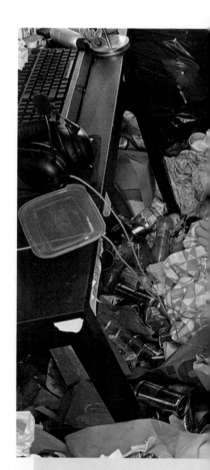

"There might even be something to do, I could go there and clean up someday," she says to me with a smile to the next one. By far the most common reason why Auri refuses a cleaning gig is because the home is too tidy. When the sender receives a negative response, they may be disappointed, but at the same time relieved that their own home is not such a hopeless case after all. Auri has indeed seen worse (i.e., in Auri's view, more wonderful).

No matter what kind of contact you make, Auri scrolls through the pictures first. The clichéd saying that a picture is worth a thousand words applies to this strategy 100 percent. Anyone can write a touching, tragic, miserable story. But when cleaning gigs are chosen by the amount of visible grime and junk shown, Auri believes that, with this strategy, she will genuinely find those who need her help the most.

Once, a Finnish-speaking woman called Auri from far away in Italy. She had reportedly hired five cleaners for her home, but not one of them knew how to keep the home in order as the woman would have liked. She inquired if Auri could come to Italy to clean and polish her

silver. Unfortunately, Auri couldn't, but wished the woman all the best and then hung up the phone.

It's obvious that some are trying to take advantage of the free-cleaning Auri. That has been the case from the beginning. On the other hand, when you think about it in more detail, each contact is a unique attempt to get the most out of Auri. What does exploitation actually mean here? After all, that's what free cleaning assistance is based on. It's built into the pattern, and that's a good thing. Anyone can ask for help.

In the pictures, Auri is looking for clutter and dirt, above all dirt. She's looking for stained cabinet doors, blackened stoves, shower walls with mold spots, grime-covered sinks. As sickening as possible (in Auri's words, wonderful), long-lasting, stuck dirt.

Garbage mountains come only second on the list, as they do not require special skills. Auri zooms in on the sequences of images that have arrived in the email and hisses when something hits her retinas. While many others would comment in a shocked tone, "How can you get an apartment in that condition?" Auri would reply, "There are numerous reasons."

"Will that apartment ever be habitable again?"

"Easily," Auri would reply.

## HOARDING IS MORE COMPLICATED

It is also necessary for Auri to look closely at the emails so as not to accidentally end up in a hoarder's home. A hoarder is a breed that Auri herself can't tame with her cleaning skills. Auri means people who are hooked on hundreds, maybe thousands, of their belongings and refuse to give them up. The overabundance of goods is accompanied by an inexplicable feeling that has nothing to do with reason or moderation. Hoarding can also be a mental illness that cannot be solved by compulsive cleaning, but requires the help of a medical professional.

Hoarders don't often ask for help; usually a loved one seeks it on their behalf. However, if Auri is invited to clean someone's home without the permission of the actual resident, perhaps at the request of a relative, the surprised party might, in the worst case, become enraged and curse Auri into the depths of the earth. Neither side would win, and everyone would be left feeling overwhelmed by forced cleaning. But in a simply dirty home, where no one would feel comfortable or able to live anymore, the situation is different. The person who lives there is rarely attached to their stains, they just can't, or don't have the strength to, get rid of them anymore.

Auri has learned to steer her work away from incurable hoarders the hard way. At one of the cleaning gigs, she made the mistake of throwing away the bedsheets, which were teeming with bed worms. It didn't occur to Auri that the resident could have missed these pieces of fabric that were in such terrible condition. However, they had so much emotional value that the person who asked for cleaning help became enraged at Auri and immediately claimed that she was a criminal. Although the situation was resolved without repercussions, Auri was brought down to earth from the experience. Today, she draws up a written agreement with the people she helps, on the basis of which she has the right to throw unusable and broken things in the trash.

### The Inbox of Sad Fates: A Selection Process

It is only after viewing the pictures that Auri reads the actual messages. These are filled with unexpected deaths of family members, sick children and animals, drug problems, rapes, cancers, prison sentences, and struggles with alcohol and mental health problems. Auri, if anyone, is always face to face with the fact that the human condition does not always taste like cotton candy. Gummy bears are not evenly distributed, and someone might just get delivered an empty package to add to their sea of trash.

> But while not everyone can be saved by a simple
> cleaning, hope for difficult situations
> may be offered to everyone.

Even though contacts come from Tampere as well as from China and India, the picture of life seen in the messages remains the same. It does not treat everyone nicely, let alone fairly. Often, the difficulties people face begin to compound, based on what Auri has experienced and seen, to accumulate on top of each other. First, someone might lose their job or spouse, maybe their credit score, and eventually the desire and ability to keep their home in a decent condition.

In other words, Auri reads stories that are each sadder than the last. However, she does not complain, or make herself believe that she can solve all the dilemmas and sorrows of the person sending the message on her own. You can't say that Auri is numb, because she has always had a practical outlook. The truth is, you can't save everyone by cleaning—that's how Auri sees it, and that's the view she also lives and works by.

But, while not everyone can be saved by a simple cleaning, hope for difficult situations may be offered to everyone. "That's why cleaning these homes is first and foremost," Auri concludes, closing the flood of messages teeming with dark fates. But soon enough, she will return to her emails a second time. It is clear that this second time will come very soon, as we have to get to the gigs even after this break.

When Auri is able to select her next cleaning site, she responds to the message and agrees on practical arrangements.

She does not make plans for the far future, but more or less for the next week. Sometimes schedules change, as the most outrageous homes often move to the head of the line. They are the most satisfying places to clean, and probably also the homes whose residents are the most in need of help. In her reply message, Auri doesn't ask any more questions, but thanks them gently for contacting her and asks when she can clean. Auri is not going to pity, advise, or judge. Auri is going to clean up.

Usually, Auri and the resident agree to exchange the keys in the yard. Then the resident goes somewhere: to run errands, or maybe to their friend's house in the next village. Some head out for a walk, if they don't have money or a close circle of friends. Only a few stay at home while Auri cleans up. Auri doesn't ask them or even worry about it, as it would slow down the cleaning process and tire the residents unreasonably. Some are outraged by simply watching from the sidelines. Some don't even want to see Auri face-to-face. They slip the keys to a neighbor, or hide them under the rug.

*Auri is not going to pity, advise, or judge.*
*Auri is going to clean up.*

All options are suitable for Auri, except for getting stood up. This has happened on one occasion when Auri had arranged a cleaning gig with a young woman. Auri had exchanged messages with her on the morning of the cleaning gig. It had been agreed that Auri would press the door buzzer. She made it all the way to the stairway, but the journey stopped at the door. Auri knocked for a while, until she gave up and returned to the car disappointed.

The woman who stood her up was heard from only later. She had reportedly forgotten that she had arranged other things for the duration of the gig. Auri was pretty sure the woman was lying to her, because the day before the cleaning, everything had seemed clear from the messages. The woman must have been ashamed of the mess in her home, or so sick that she didn't realize what a nasty trick she had done by taking Auri's time away from someone who would have accepted help. However, normally, if everything goes according to plan, Auri opens the door to the apartment and gets inside. She wanders around the house, humming approvingly. Then things start to happen.

# Expectation Vs. Reality

## *Operation Garbage*

First a landfill, then a habitable, tidy home. First brown mud and wet debris, then bright and shiny porcelain. The extremes change with a snap of the fingers—that's what happens in the videos. Music plays, and the home turns into an ordinary, homey-looking home. Everything has been made to look effortless, but the reality is different.

On average, cleaning gigs take Auri about twenty hours. The hours are typically spread over two days, and at noon Auri goes to lunch or orders food. In the middle of the gig, she sips caffeine-free Nocco and scoops nuts into her mouth. Sometimes more time passes and sometimes less, especially if Auri has been helped by Anni, her brother Santeri, or someone else close to her. The assistants have learned techniques and efficiency from Auri, so she is happy to take them with her. If the apartment's dirtiness surprises her only on arrival, Auri might ask for help on her Instagram account. When Auri was doing a cleaning gig in Vaasa, six of her followers enthusiastically rushed to carry garbage bags.

In relation to the rest of the work, it takes a mercilessly long time to simply throw rubbish in the trash. Auri strives to sort cardboard and paper, but she does not have the capacity to engage in thorough recycling. The residents also discuss in advance what they want to save and what can be thrown away without regret. Despite this, Auri sometimes has to send the resident pictures of the items she encounters and ask what their verdict is: in the trash or in storage?

Recently, Auri was cleaning with her little brother. "This looks so easy in the videos," her brother quipped, after collecting rubbish for who knows how long.

In reality, it is a painfully long-winded operation consisting of a single, repetitive movement. It's frustrating if the rubbish doesn't find its way into the garbage bag and rolls back onto the floor. Most of your hand muscles are strained by glass jars, which may have mold inside. When you pick up the trash, you don't know if you're going to come across a battalion of bugs, some smelly liquid, or takeout food that has started walking out of its box. The most memorable has been a half-empty 1.5-liter bottle of Pepsi, which was in the refrigerator. Although the drink was stored in the cold, it had still begun to grow mold.

It is also not possible to record in the videos the smell that hovers in the apartment. The mere aromas in her nose reveal the true state of things to Auri. If you get a stale scent in the apartment, there is probably no wet or hidden dirt that can be recognized by a more pungent smell. According to Auri, the smell could also be described as rotten. It's the smell of decaying dirt, a stench that takes over the whole space. You get used to it, but notice it again if you return after stepping out for a while.

Auri is not disgusted, no matter how strong the smell is. She may have a weaker sense of smell than usual, which may be caused by the strong chemicals used in cleaning work. However, it's often different for the people who help her. Once, Auri and a friend were cleaning a place where dirty dishes had been standing in a damp bathroom for two years. When the friend grabbed the dishes and started washing them, the smell was so pervasive that he vomited in his mouth.

"This looks so easy in the videos."

An additional spice to the job is brought by taking the trash to the garbage bins. It is a physically strenuous hike, which is not made any easier if the house lacks an elevator or the bins are hundreds of meters away. However, it is not unusual for a neighbor to recognize Auri, then call the tenant's landlord or property manager in a hurry.

The worst fear for some is that the amount of trash from a one-time cleaning will cause an additional fee for other residents. Even if it did, it probably would be only a couple of euros.

This happened once, when Auri was cleaning the apartment of a girl who had just barely turned eighteen. The neighbor, who was guarding the windows and the yard, was so distraught by the amount of trash collected from the apartment that he finally rushed to the scene and started yelling at Auri in the face. A neighbor yelled at a woman who was cleaning for free and scolded her for being irresponsible. When the landlord arrived, accompanied by a neighbor, he, too, was at first worried about who would pay for the removal of the trash. Auri held her ground and calmly explained what it was all about, and why there was an unimaginable amount of rubbish.

"What if we together tried to help this girl? She is only eighteen," she suggested to the fuming duo.

Eventually, the landlord took Auri's side. After calming down, he even thanked her for the work she was doing. However, the situation left its mark on Auri's way of cleaning up. Now, in case of future crises, Auri tries to keep as low a profile as possible when the road leads to a new destination. She doesn't want to get tenants in trouble, especially since it is already challenging enough to clean homes to make them habitable again.

For example, before marching to the trash bins, Auri might check whether the route is clear. Then she sneaks in, and disappears just as quickly. If there is an exceptionally large amount of trash, Auri calls the property manager, informs them about the situation, and asks them to send the invoice directly to her company.

### The Most Annoying Part Ever

The final videos you see online never reveal how harsh and strenuous the practical tweaking of their filming has been. When the tripods of two cameras and a flash are connected with wires to an apartment flooded with debris, the chaos is complete. At first, Auri shoots with one camera, then another, and lastly with her phone. The starting position must be captured on TikTok, YouTube, and Instagram in slightly different ways. Videos and images of an unclean home must be taken from exactly the same angle as similar shots of the cleaned home, so that the viewer believes they are comparable.

Sami and Anni, who have both accompanied Auri on dozens of cleaning gigs, say that adjusting the filming setups is the most painful phase. You can't start cleaning, or even prepare, until you've made sure the starting point is stored in the camera's memory.

Auri admits that sometimes filming annoys her too. It eats up a lot of time and makes the starting point of a cleaning gig a big deal. Once, it happened to Auri that five cleaning gigs were completely invisible to viewers due to damaged image quality. At the first gig, the camera crashed. Auri didn't realize at the time that something had broken inside the device, so she kept working as usual. It wasn't until Auri's editor, Nea, started going through the videos that it became clear that the image was as fuzzy as could be.

"It was just a messy blur," Auri recalls. Cleaning the lens didn't solve the problem, so Auri had to visit camera shops. But, like an omen of fate, the new camera crashed immediately on its maiden gig. Auri couldn't believe her luck—or what an airhead she can sometimes be. Fortunately, only the lens broke down that time, and the structure of the camera was not damaged.

If Auri could choose, she would focus solely on cleaning and let someone else handle the videotaping. So far, this has not been practically possible. Fortunately, imagining what the video will look like later motivates her to memorize the details carefully. After all, it is satisfying to look at them afterwards yourself.

### The Illusion of Being Finished

According to her assistants, Auri is a master at estimating the time that a cleaning is going to take. Anni remembers how, at the first gigs, she was overwhelmed by the feeling that the end would never be reached. She couldn't believe Auri, who assured them that the gig would take about seven hours. At the end of the day, however, the clock reported that six hours and fifty-five minutes had passed. After being on a cleaning gig with Auri, I can understand where Anni's concern came from. In short: I feel you, sis.

In addition to precise time management, Auri has rules for the order of the work. When Sami, who loves to organize, has been involved in a gig, he has sometimes started to pick up books lying in the hallway in a nearby closet. Not long ago, he got a mouthful from Auri, who said that that work was not worth doing then, since the order was wrong. As you explore more of the apartment, a bookshelf may be revealed, as has often been the case.

At the end of the gig, Auri usually buys something for the resident. Sometimes it's a houseplant, other times it's new sheets or a mattress pad to replace an old one that is flooded with insects that have spread from food waste. Especially in cases where Auri has had to leave only the light in the fridge after emptying it, she may buy fruits, vegetables, or ready-made salads, for example. She doesn't add condiments to the cabinets, because people have enough of them anyway (and sometimes, if you ask Auri, too many).

One other thing the videos don't reveal is that the home will never actually be perfectly finished. This first became clear to me during one of our joint cleaning gigs, when we moved cardboard boxes of videocassettes, a clothesline with laundry on it, and a bunch of electronics to the balcony. It's clear that Auri doesn't show up to turn water into wine and go through every cupboard, down to the darkest corner. The final fate of the goods in the home and their arrangement remains the responsibility of the resident. However, when the apartment is clean, things are much more painless to go through, if only because they're no longer drowned in a sea of trash.

A very precise person should consider another job description.

"Auri is accurate, but not too precise," says best friend Anni. "If we're at a cleaning gig together, Auri is the one who says we don't have time for that. I remember thinking earlier, what will the resident think if this or that is left undone? At that point, you have to recall the initial situation. This person has lived in total turmoil, so it is hardly a big deal if you leave a box of dishes unwashed or a stain on the wall."

In other words, Auri takes care of the cleaning gigs according to the available time. You don't always have to do the same thing— it's enough to clean up what you can, have time for, and want to. If it takes hours to move things around, it's because of arranging cabinets and washing dishes. The most important thing for Auri is that the surfaces are cleaned, and that the apartment is in a livable condition for the residents' everyday life.

Sometimes Auri has also been accompanied by incurable perfectionists. If they are asked to wipe a cat-sized stain from the wall, it will be difficult to leave it unwiped. Somewhere else—say, at the back of a closet or at the ceiling line, there is another, third, fourth stain, which, in the opinion of a perfectionist, would also call for the clean touch of a microfiber towel. In other words: a very precise person should consider another job description.

"If I was a perfectionist and wanted to achieve the perfect result, I wouldn't be able to clean up these homes. You can't clean them up so that they're immaculate. If the resident hasn't seen their floor for years, like a monk, cleaners should let go in a reasonable amount of time and let it be," Auri sums up.

# The Bombest Home of All Time

It was the most amazing thing Auri had ever seen. She found it hard to believe that the bathroom even existed. The sight was so breathtakingly beautiful to Auri that she couldn't take her eyes off the picture.

First of all, the entire shower room was thoroughly blackened. One could have imagined from its color that pitch had been thrown on the floor. The difference between the floor and the white wall tiles visible nearby seemed dreamlike, or the result of image editing. No previous cleaning gig had reached anywhere near the same level. Due to the clogging of the drain, water stood on the floor like a small pond.

Looking at the picture, Auri could almost sense how bacteria were munching on their foods all over the bathroom. The kitchen was covered with greasy, persistent dirt. The resident certainly cooked for himself and didn't just order takeout; that's how polluted and used the kitchen looked.

Both the sticky grime in the bathroom and the stained cabinets in the kitchen seemed to scream Auri's name. Auri knew she had to get there.

Photos of the bomb-ridden apartment had come from afar, from a Swiss country village. They had been sent by a woman a few years younger than Auri, whom we can call Nora. Nora hadn't been able to clean her apartment in over six years.

Auri decided to have a video call with Nora. During that call, Nora shared her life story. The downturn had started quite suddenly, but typically: after getting fired. In 2014, Nora was fired, after which she sank into severe depression. She had stopped going outside and had frozen relations with almost all of her friends. She was left lying in her bed, and had squandered her characteristically Swiss, sizable unemployment allowance by shopping online to make herself feel better. She covered up her melancholy by binging on boxes of pizza. At some point, Nora had even cut her hair off completely, so that she wouldn't have to take a shower to wash it anymore.

Nora hadn't let anyone inside her home in years. But when she was suddenly hospitalized for her physical problems, the parents had been tipped off about the condition of the apartment. The mother yelled at her daughter for indolence, and couldn't fathom how she could have destroyed the rented apartment in such a horrible way.

After being discharged from the hospital, Nora decided to move in with her brother. Soon she would have to give up her apartment. The landlord had no idea of the state the apartment was in. *Is there anything that could be done?* she wondered. Nora invited a cleaning company to take a look at the situation and give her an estimate for cleaning the apartment. It was revealed that the cleaning would cost more than 15,000 euros. Needless to say, an unemployed woman could not possibly afford it.

Since Nora knew about Auri's existence at the time, she decided to try what seemed impossible: to get help from far-away Finland. *There would be nothing to lose, even if I just sent a message,* Nora thought.

When Auri saw the pictures and heard the story, she wanted to fly to Nora the very same day. Auri quickly wrote a message to her main sponsor, who promised to pay Auri and Sami to travel to Switzerland. A week went by, and the pair were in the skies over Europe with suitcases full of cleaning supplies. Auri was afraid that there wouldn't be a cleaning gig, and Scrub Daddy's management would be grumpy. She knew she had taken a risk by going thousands of miles away for a gig. Fortunately, the apartment did exist. Auri and Sami met Nora on her street and soon went in together. Nora couldn't believe that Auri was actually in her apartment.

Auri and Sami, on the other hand, could not believe what they saw. There are apartments that seem promising, but are revealed to be a disappointment on the spot. Too neat. That home really wasn't. It was everything Auri had dreamed of, and more.

There were spiders shivering on the floor, braiding cobwebs all over the apartment, and living inside hundreds of empty pizza boxes. The blockage that had taken over the bathroom drain had spread across the threshold into the living room, which could be seen from the brown boundary line drawn there. And then, ah, those piles of clothes. The damp clothes were glued to the ground, and when you tried to lift them, they tore into tiny bits of fabric.

From the extreme details, it seemed that time had been allowed to gnaw the surfaces of the apartment freely for years. Sami, who was also used to bomb homes, was terrified. Actually, he didn't touch any of the surfaces in the apartment, which made the cleaning complicated. When it got hot, Sami took off his hoodie in the stairwell and left it there.

He refused to put the shirt on any of the surfaces in the apartment. With its spiders and stains, it gave him chills. Sami felt like he had gotten lost at the scene of a murder. How could such a warm, ordinary-looking girl have lived in a scene like a horror movie? Wasn't Nora scared to live here?

When Auri and Sami started cleaning, Nora's brother was also there. The brother couldn't believe that the cleaners who had arrived from Finland would have the slightest chance of succeeding and getting the apartment in order. Nora told Auri about her brother's educated guesses. Then she went on to say that she fully believed in Auri because she had watched her videos. "But I just thought I'd say," Nora whispered.

It was the first cleaning gig where Auri had to wear a mask. So much dust from the damp, lumpy clothes was released into the air that even a hardened cleaner like her could not breathe the air there without protection.

What was similar to other sites was that most of the cleaning time was spent fighting with garbage. It took one full day.

Switzerland is such a special country that the color of your garbage bags depends on where in the country you live. That is, the waste must be put in a bag of a certain color in one area, and another color in another. In addition, one can be fined for bringing in too much rubbish from one household for disposal. The rules of the game didn't quite make sense to Auri and Sami, but what they understood was that the garbage business in Switzerland was different from the one at home.

Auri, Sami, and Nora wondered how to solve the problem. In the end, Nora's brother agreed to pick up and transport the garbage with a tractor that he had access to. Attached to it was a large trailer, with high sides which prevented debris from spilling out. More than a hundred garbage bags were accumulated for the tractor to transport. Before that, they had time to fill the balcony twice.

The cleaning took a total of four days. In other words, it was Auri's longest-duration cleaning gig to date. However, on the last day, Auri and Sami mainly focused on shooting the end result for the videos. A pretty-looking home of more than eighty square meters had emerged from under the filth. There were particularly fine stone floors. Suddenly, the two of them were standing in an apartment where one could imagine some high-income business person, or even a small family, living.

Nora had a hard time believing her eyes. In the end, she managed to move out of the apartment without the landlord ever knowing what condition it had been in. That's how clean Auri and Sami had gotten it. When Nora's mother arrived, she gratefully forced a gift package on Auri and Sami, into which she had also slipped a thank-you letter. Auri would have been happy with just the end results.

Switzerland and Nora were just the beginning of conquering foreign countries. Since then, Auri has been cleaning or has plans to in Sweden, Germany, the UK, and the US. They are not noticeably different from domestic gigs, except that cleaning products cannot be taken on board, but must be purchased at the destination. Cleaning and filming equipment will follow Auri's journey, but she must bring a helper with her on every trip, since she can't transport all of it by herself.

## Gratitude and Something Completely Different

The trip to Switzerland was memorable in every possible way. In addition to the fact that the gig was done far from home, the apartment had been in a wilder condition than any of the previous locations in Finland. Finally, Nora was absolutely intoxicated by the help she had received.

However, the success of a gig is not determined by how a person reacts to the outcome, or whether they keep in touch later. Auri does not choose the apartments to be cleaned according to whether there is chemistry with the resident.

Still, she admits that hearing praise feels good—like once, when she was cleaning the home of a woman in a wheelchair. Auri arrived at the apartment and immediately received a bouquet of flowers from the woman in the hallway. She had been, completely unexpectedly, confined to a wheelchair a year and a half earlier, and it had triggered depression. The doctors couldn't tell her why her legs were failing, and she had to learn to cope with that fact.

The woman told Auri that she had always dreamed of going into the army. It had been her biggest dream. Now the wheelchair had thwarted that intention, and made it difficult to keep her home in order. Despite the depression, there was something sunny about her. And there was all the more gratitude when she got to see her tidy home at the end of the gig.

*It was once neat and clean here.*
*It can be neat and clean here again.*

But not all gigs start with a bouquet, let alone end with tears of joy. Auri often does not get a hug or hear a thank you. Some people don't seem terribly interested that she has come to clean their home, even though they contacted her themselves. Auri understands the reaction well, and believes that the cause may be mental health problems, such as depression, or the fact that the person denies what has happened, or downplays it in their mind as minor. Once Auri was cleaning a young man's apartment with Sami. For Sami, the smell of the gig was especially memorable. The way the apartment smelled, already, from the elevator, thus proved they had reached the right floor. Since it was a hot July, the scent of biowaste inside the apartment had spread all the way to the stairwell.

The most distinctive detail of the apartment was the almost absurd number of dirty dishes. There were about five hundred dirty dishes; they would have been enough for the needs of the entire building. Mold had begun to grow on them. Apparently, the man had never washed the dishes, but when he ate off a plate or sipped out of a mug, he had thrown the dishes into a plastic box, to hide like garbage to be taken away. While the pair were washing dishes, drying, and washing dishes again, the man was spinning around in the apartment. At one point, Auri talked to him and asked how it felt to get help. "Does it make you feel better?"

"It doesn't really feel like anything," the man replied, shrugging.

Auri cannot, and does not want to, demand fireworks from people. There is no sacred promise that after the cleaning work, their life will change and they will start to take care of the apartment. Thinking about what the apartment will look like in a week or a year is pointless for Auri, and would take away the joy of cleaning.

But if there is anything left for the resident, it is at least a memory of what the home has sometimes looked like, when it was tidy. Perhaps some will cherish it and gain hope from it: *It was once neat and clean here. It can be neat and clean here again.*

At times, people are ungrateful. For example, one time children contacted Auri and asked her for help on behalf of their parents, initially behind their parents' backs. When Auri arrived at the house, she ended up cleaning just the downstairs for eight hours. That was all she could do. The children's sleeping places were there, and Auri had found some dried cat droppings in the beds. Even though the pets were wandering around the apartment, they had made it a habit to go and do their business in the children's room.

When the ground floor started to look more habitable, and Auri was finishing the gig, the parents were scolding her. Instead of giving thanks, they wondered if the person who had come to clean wasn't going to clean the whole house. "Couldn't you put the whole house in order, since you've dragged yourself all the way here?" However, Auri did not do that. For this gig, she had the time (and the desire) to help only those who had asked her for help.

*Just as easily, you might be faced with a gentle, warm, bubbly, and ordinary person who has simply been through hard times in one way or another.*

Then there are those gigs that, so to speak, rise to other dimensions. Once Auri was actually scared to go on a gig, even though she had a friend with her. The destination was a terraced (row) house in a small town. The house was a base for those struggling with drug problems. The residents who had asked for help behaved unpredictably, and a little suspiciously, when they met. The cinematic nature of the gig was topped off by the knowledge that the home was full of stolen goods. While cleaning, Auri had some restless thoughts. *If we get killed now, then we get killed, and nothing can be done about it.*

Auri is aware that she takes a risk every time she goes to clean. Imagine, every time you are faced with someone you've never met before, who can be of any kind—harsh, offensive, or threatening. Mentally shaken, criminal, or with substance abuse problems. Or, just as easily, you might be faced with a gentle, warm, bubbly, and ordinary person who has simply been through hard times in one way or another.

Auri went through the most bewildering scenarios in her mind right before her first cleaning gig. She realized that she could not prepare for threatening situations with special precautions or tricks. There is no questionnaire that can secure your back and make you sure that things won't go badly at the gig. You have to trust that people, no matter what they have done, will appreciate the person who cleans voluntarily, so that they do not attack them.

In any case, at a cleaning gig, Auri often has a friend with her, for example, Anni, Santeri, or some of her followers. Especially men's homes, she doesn't like to clean alone. On the other hand, she has noticed that, when Sami is involved in a gig, the men are always less talkative and deliberately avoid contact. They don't open up about their situation as boldly as if Auri were there alone.

One of the most off-putting gigs was when Auri went to clean a single father's home. Hanging on the wall there were large, sharp-looking knives and pictures of Russian President Vladimir Putin. Auri cut them out of sight in the video, as the pictures would have taken attention away from cleaning up. Be that as it may, the story of that home was tragic in every way. The single parent had emailed Auri about his daughter, who had been raped by someone in their own apartment.

At first, the father had not been able to clean the particular room where it had happened. In the end, he was too anxious to take care of the apartment at all.

This gig of cleaning the home of a potential criminal or suspects isn't the only one of its kind. People don't mention the crimes in their contacts, but they seem to Auri like open letters. The thought is unsophisticated and hard to avoid.

On one occasion, in addition to other suspicious elements, the resident had already been evicted from his home. He probably could have left it alone, but he decided to ask Auri for help.

For Auri, it does not matter whether the person living in the apartment has done something wrong in their life, or lived completely according to the norms of society. Things are never so black and white. People are neither thoroughly evil nor good. Auri does not consider it her job or her right to judge those in need. It would also be unnecessary from the point of view of her mission.

## Operation Snow Shovel

Although Auri cleans an average of one home a week, it took a long time for a world-class bomb target to turn up domestically—an apartment that surpassed even the Swiss destination.

The current jackpot hit in July 2022. In western Finland, there was a large, abandoned-looking detached house, whose occupant said in an email that she had attempted suicide.

In another, earlier email, she had said her girlfriend had left. Auri found a third email in which the resident said that her move was approaching, which is why she desperately needed cleaning help. The actual justification for cleaning remained unclear, but one thing was certain: there would be enough clutter and dirt. The most recent email was accompanied by three telling images that sealed Auri's decision.

A cousin who had previously worked for Auri's mother's cleaning company and under Auri agreed to be her travel companion. Auri was also able to attract three other followers who wanted to join, one of whom came all the way from Tampere. Lastly, before leaving,

Auri decided to call the resident and make sure that the property would really be as good as the pictures.

"It is," a voice from the end of the phone assured her. "There are rats buzzing here again," she continued.

Instead of shying away from what she heard, Auri got even more excited. The rat problem suggested the apartment was screaming for a thorough cleaning.

Soon, Auri and her cousin made their way into a yard that resembled a jungle. The lawn was uncut, and there was stuff, rubbish, and boxes everywhere in mounds. It quickly dawned on Auri that the yard really was just a prelude.

"This is the worst, or the loveliest, place I've ever been to," she realized as she walked around inside.

The occupant had almost no teeth. Auri decided to ask directly if she was using drugs. The woman assured her that she was not and that she only suffered from mental health problems. Then she lit a cigarette and offered to make coffee. When Auri and the cousin didn't want the coffee, the resident made a mug for herself. After drinking it, she plunged into the garage, which was full of stuff as well. She had to clear a way for herself there.

When Auri took a closer look at the apartment, she noticed that there were heaps of partially intact and partly rotten things, including loose furniture, among the rubbish. However, there was so much rubbish that Auri decided to get a waste pallet for the site. It was hard to get hold of the trash pallet. Several companies that

Auri called said no and told her about their two-week waiting lists. In the end, Auri caught up with an entrepreneur who promised to bring a skip to the yard.

When the skip problem was solved, Auri and her cousin set about emptying the apartment with a snow shovel. The sturdy shovel was more effective than the usual working tool, gloved hands. In Auri's opinion, shoveling was the best thing ever. At one point, she asked the resident if she could also throw unusable stuff that had turned into rubbish on the garbage pallet. The resident said that, for herself, getting rid of the goods would be suitable, but for her girlfriend it was something else. Her girlfriend? Auri was confused.

Weren't they broken up? And if they really lived together here, where did they actually sleep? There was only one sofa in the house, no bed or a place that even remotely resembled one. It soon became clear that the couple also had another apartment, where the girlfriend was now staying, and where this person was going to move.

Auri worried about the attitude of the girlfriend. Her internal radar said they were facing a hoarder, which would create an additional challenge for the cleaning.

When the resident made a video call to the girlfriend and pointed the camera at a rotten stool, the girlfriend exclaimed that it should not be thrown away, of course. "Absolutely not," she said, and that was that.

In the end, almost all the broken and dirty things she wanted to keep had to be carried in cardboard boxes in the pouring rain. Auri felt like she was on a hidden camera, or in a skit. She almost found herself hoping that heavy rain would destroy the things beyond recognition so that they, too, would find their way to where they belonged: the garbage.

The ultimate sign of hoarding was the kitchen; it had not been accessible for more than three years. It was so full of stuff that you simply couldn't walk in there. Another example was a tall cabinet that blocked the corridor of the apartment. And not just any corridor, but the one that gave the only access to the shower and sauna in the place.

The resident, who stayed in the garage for the duration of the gig, told Auri that she hadn't been able to wash herself in the house for three years. Despite the hoarding, Auri experienced satisfaction as they gradually opened up the space and progressed from room to room. Even the droppings left by the rats, which Auri had not come across before, played merely a supporting role in the meditative snow shovel operation.

The flow of cleaning was interrupted on the second day when the owner of the apartment, Maija, who was almost eighty, knocked on the door. Auri and her assistants had gotten to cleaning the kitchen, so the worst of the clearing was behind them. Maija walked around the house and couldn't really say anything. She wandered around the apartment, looking around, and uttering one phrase over and over again.

"How is it like this in here? Do I need to do some renovation?" she repeated. Auri had to tell her that the house could not be made habitable just by cleaning. The rats had defecated everywhere and chewed the electrical wires to bits. The landlord's shock did nosubside. Then, suddenly, she was gone. The resident, who was in the garage, soon came in and cursed the landlord's behavior.

"How dare she come here and complain," the resident sighed, sounding bored. Although Auri was haunted by the chain of events, she continued to clean up with her sidekicks.

The next day, Maija arrived again, this time with her daughter. First of all, they thanked Auri profusely and asked to help. Although Auri assured them that she didn't need help, they still stayed for a while to watch the cleanup. During the chat, Auri found out what had happened.

Maija's daughter had seen on social media that Auri had asked for cleaning help in their hometown. When Auri posted videos of the bomb room, kitchen tiling had revealed to Maija that it was the home she owned. Without seeing the kitchen tiles, she would not have recognized the house as her own—a house that she had built with her husband, and in which she had lived for more than forty years. After her husband died, she had rented her home out to its current residents.

Maija hadn't been able to get into the living space since then, even though she had tried at some point. The tenants had aroused her suspicions a long time ago, and she had persistently tried to get rid of them. When that hadn't worked out, she had resigned herself to the situation. Maija had convinced herself that maybe the house would be okay, even though the yard looked so shocking. Perhaps the residents took the trash to the yard so that they could live a normal everyday life inside. Now this belief has been proven wrong.

Despite the turnaround, Auri continued to clean up. For a total of three days, she, her cousin, and her followers diligently cleaned up. The operation was accelerated by ordering a waste pallet and the fact that everything could be carried outside, unlike in apartment buildings. Although the cleaning team worked hard, the job wasn't finished.

For example, they did not have time to interfere with (or even enter) the shower and sauna. Still, the cleaning was satisfying, rewarding, and even fun.

It seemed especially meaningful to do a favor for the homeowner, Maija—a lovely, and a little too naïve, old woman whose long-term home had turned into a house of horrors at the hands of tenants. Making it habitable, probably with the help of professionals, was going to take a toll on Maija's time and strength, if it was even possible now.

A few months later, Auri learned that Maija had convinced the tenants to leave because they had failed to pay the rent. Now Maija spends time in the apartment, opening walls and floors, and has also called a plumber and an electrician. She even managed to make her way to the shower that no one had been to for three years. Maija would like to get the house back in order so that she could sell it, or maybe rent it out again. However, it may just as well happen that a rat-damaged building can no longer be a residential building. Time will tell.

# Reading the Signs

Although Auri concentrates her energy and interest on the dirt during her gigs, even she doesn't clean up without noticing the people. After visiting more than a hundred messy homes, you start to notice small and bigger details. What is repeated frequently in these homes? What kinds of things do the people who desperately need Auri's help have in common?

By far, Auri cleans small homes the most, especially one-room and two-room apartments in blocks of flats. In many cases, they are rental apartments. And when cleaning apartments of scanty square meters, it is very likely that they are the homes of those who live alone. Of course, sometimes Auri makes acquaintances even with messy family apartments, and it is not unusual to meet a couple or a single parent with one or more children.

Auri remembers once cleaning a room in a shared apartment. All the common areas were tip-top, but the room of the person who needed cleaning help was a mess. The resident had stacked a pile of mattresses on the floor as a substitute for a bed, as none of the mattresses could fit in the real bed frame. The bed frame stood bare amidst the mess. Auri tried asking for someone on social media to donate a suitable mattress. When the mattress was not immediately found, she decided to use her creativity and use scissors to cut the cleanest mattress into a smaller one.

Such cases are rare, among the large number of people living alone that Auri has cleaned for. However, those who live alone are not carved from the same wood. They may be students living in a single apartment, widowed or sick elderly people, those who have lost control of their lives. Some keep their scenes in order and some don't have the energy to perform, at least not for Auri. Some have a lot of close relationships, but some have none.

When you live alone, you are responsible exclusively for yourself. Then the standard of cleanliness in the home may easily go down. Or, even the height of the bar can be determined by one who lives alone. And then, at some point, that bar disappears completely. No one notices that it is no longer swinging in place.

If you suffer from clutter and dirt alone and don't care about yourself, what does it matter? Perhaps the apartment will never be visited by strangers. A food courier can leave an order at the door without having to exchange a word. Many of those who have contacted Auri say they have had such thoughts. Loneliness is not always easy to detect, but unremedied, it can cause a home to silently fall into a state of chaos.

Among Auri's cleaning gigs, there aren't many apartments where her rubber-gloved hands haven't touched payment reminders, enforcement forms, and overdue credit card bills. Sometimes they have been read, torn, and pushed aside. They lie dormant in the depths of shelves or under the garbage. At times, completely untouched and unopened, they have been allowed to multiply freely into an ever higher and taller stack.

In addition to bills, she is often faced with notes that indicate unemployment. These are, for example, Kela's (Finnish social insurance) decisions on social assistance granted, or invitations from the municipality to rehabilitative work trials. On the other hand, many people have day jobs.

*Loneliness is not always easy to detect, but unremedied, it can cause a home to silently fall into a state of chaos.*

Such was the young woman who contacted Auri via Instagram. The profile was bursting with pictures of an exceptionally beautiful and fit person who earned a living as an entrepreneur in the fitness business.

The comment sections were filled with admiring words. From everything visible, it seemed that the woman had friends, and even fans. At the cleaning gig, Auri paid particular attention to the paintings hanging in the middle of the mess. They were embroidered with uplifting phrases, calligraphy-lettered advice to believe in oneself and be happy.

In Auri's opinion, it is unnecessary to make assumptions about the cleanliness or uncleanliness of anyone's home. Losing control of one's life is a complex maze, and Auri doesn't try to explain it to others or to herself. Similarly, it may be the case that someone shows symptoms of feeling unwell by cleaning obsessively. Auri is not a psychologist, but a cleaner who does what she knows how to do: clean and arrange the home.

In any case, even more common than unemployment and economic hardship are the mental health problems of residents. In addition to people's own stories, Auri is informed by the medicine bottles found in the apartment and the tablets lying loose on the floor. Antidepressants, pills that affect mood or curb insomnia, and empty liquor bottles are a familiar sight for Auri as she goes from one apartment to another.

*No one's life story should be guessed at, or even assumed. Everyone has their battles.*

While the young and depressed Auri wandered restlessly from place to place, and could sometimes arrange her belongings in a closet, depression made time stand still. A bed flooded with empty food parcels speaks to the fact that, on the worst days, the resident has not been able to get out of bed. The image of a depressed person who has lost all zest for life may be a one-sided stereotype, but at Auri's cleaning gigs, it is an everyday reality.

And then there is the food. By food, Auri does not mean oatmeal, bags of bread, skinned potatoes, or frozen foods. Instead, on cleaning gigs, people she helps often eat fast food. There are cardboard bags from McDonald's and Hesburger, another fast-food chain in Finland, pizza boxes in the colors of the Italian flag, or microwavable pizzas from Saarioinen, a Finnish convenience food company. At this point, "junk" food is an accurate descriptor, because in these apartments, the existence of food is evidenced by plastic and cardboard wrappers, which have become nothing more than rubbish in the sea of garbage. There may also be intoxicants in the apartments, but not nearly as likely as unpaid bills, various medicines, and empty or half-eaten fast-food packages.

When a person's mental health fails and money runs out, it rarely happens without reason. Some suffer from physical pain that has taken away the ability to hold things together. Terrible things may have happened along the way, such as the death of a child or a sudden divorce, which plunge them into sudden darkness. It is not surprising that a difficult situation is reflected in the home, where a person is at their most vulnerable.

Messy homes are everywhere. In large and small towns, in rundown suburbs and more developed areas, even in upscale blocks. Auri interacts with neglected and very real homes, often for weeks. I don't think Auri will be shocked by anything she hears anymore, no matter how abominable or tragic a chain of events is.

Facing the horrors has taught Auri that no one's life story should be guessed at, or even assumed. Everyone has their battles, and those battles put their stamp on us in different ways. Some begin to overperform or overwork, others live and breathe through intoxicants. Others allow their homes to develop into landfills where ordinary life is out of the question.

## Changing the Lives of the Young and Old

Auri has noticed slight differences in cleaning gigs, based, for example, on whether the resident is a man or a woman. If cleaning gigs are representative, men often stuff their nooks and crannies full of movies, games, and electronics like backup screens, broken phones, dozens of cables, headphones, and empty device packs. With women, the objects of hoarding are likely to be of a different kind. There is makeup, jewelry, perfume bottles, kilotons of clothes and accessories collected from supermarkets, and collectibles, which are available for free when you subscribe to a magazine.

While Auri receives messages equally from all genders, the situation is different when it comes to age. After all, the majority of those who send her messages are young people. One of them was twenty-four-year-old Juho, whose home Auri ended up cleaning. Juho told Auri about his parents, who had been heavy consumers of drugs and alcohol throughout the boy's childhood. Pretty quickly, Juho had started using intoxicants himself. He had also been convicted of drunk driving, and became seriously indebted. The situation had turned hopeless.

Despite this, Juho had sought a debt counselor and decided to get things right, including in his home. It was a lucky coincidence when Auri answered him. Juho did not stay to watch Auri clean up, but disappeared for a couple of days. In the meantime, Auri had finished everything, and when he returned, the apartment looked as it had at its peak. Suddenly, Juho, who had been hiding under his hard shell, melted and burst into tears. He rushed to hug Auri.

Young people are part of the so-called Instagram generation. They haven't been able to escape the streams of images showing well-groomed homes decorated with floral arrangements, trendy pillows, and candles. The Instagram generation knows exactly what society expects from them and their apartments. While some have become blind to the uncleanliness of their homes, this has rarely happened to young people. On the contrary: they are even the most ashamed. They have a need to explain and apologize for the sight that Auri encounters when she opens the door. They are worried about what kind of impression they will make on Auri. At that point, no matter how much Auri assures the resident that she is not blaming or passing judgment on them, it doesn't help. It doesn't help if you go on to say that, for Auri, this sight is as ordinary as a tidy everyday home, which we apologize for the state of if guests happen to stop by.

In addition to young people, Auri has also encountered some of the older generation, such as Leila, an eighty-six-year-old with memory loss. She suffers from Alzheimer's disease, so Auri had been contacted by her offspring. Leila lives in a spacious, eighty-square-meter apartment. She has lived in it almost all her adult life, first with her husband and then, widowed, alone. The pictures of the apartment were promising, but not so bad that Auri would have thought she needed helpers. At that time, Auri was still working her day job, so she booked only one Saturday for the cleaning gig. On Sunday, she had planned to relax before the upcoming workweek.

It wasn't until she arrived at the apartment early in the morning that the truth was revealed. The apartment was really bad, as Auri describes it. The kitchen was covered in black rot. Instead of packets of fast food, the home was filled with bags of bread that had passed their best days, and those crumbs that Leila wasn't able to sweep away anymore. When Auri forwarded a picture of the apartment to Anni, she immediately offered to come to her aid. So did Auri's former coworker, who was enthusiastic about what she saw. Suddenly, Auri was assisted by two hard-working friends. By working together, they got the home in order in one day.

Leila was there all day. She hid from the cleaners and couldn't seem to understand what was going on around her. Leila sat on the couch while Auri sorted the trash, took it to the garbage bin, and started scrubbing the surfaces. The longer Auri cleaned, the more refreshed Leila's appearance became. When Auri and her friends were ready, Leila miraculously returned to the present day. She told Auri how she had lived in her home for over thirty-six years and remembered vividly that this was what the kitchen had looked like, this was how she had actually lived. Auri felt like she was playing an old, memory-flooded song for a memory-impaired person. A clean home brought Leila back for a while.

# Lights Out in Your Own Home

Imagine your own home sickening you so much that you can't even keep the lights on. You move there in the darkness, except in the bathroom, where you have to be able to see properly.

For Alli, this was not a bad dream, but real life. She was in her thirties, a former alcoholic whose ten-year-old son had been taken into custody several years earlier. After a long period of treatment and rehabilitation, Alli had overcome the liquor devil and given up the bottle altogether.

Child welfare services had promised that the boy could return home and Alli would get custody back for herself, as long as the place became habitable again.

All seventy square meters of the home reminded Alli of how sick and confused she had been. It was embarrassing and sickening. Beer bottles blocked the way to the dining table. Broken dressers and chairs were lying in pieces on the floor. Beer cans had also taken their place in the bathroom sink. The boy's room was like a dumpster, and the bed there was teeming with bed worms. Everything should have been thrown away and replaced, but Alli couldn't do it.

> If the viewer of the video shudders,
> imagine how the person who lives there feels.

The only place where she could somehow make her time go by was the bed in her own bedroom. There she lay, and hoped that the home would clean itself. When she explained the situation to her child, he suggested something crazy at first.

"There's a girl on TikTok who cleans homes for free. Invite her here," the boy said.

Alli found Auri's videos, and soon she had the courage to write an email to Auri, who was immediately inspired by her contact.

"After Auri has gone to clean, I wonder if I can invite friends to come visit us?" the boy asked when he heard the happy news from his mother. Alli thought that might well be the case.

At the cleaning gig, Auri was greeted by a thoughtful and kind, clean, and normal-looking young woman. The only crack in the pattern was the wildly messy home, which Alli still could barely stand to look at herself. She walked away while cleaning, and suggested Auri throw everything away without thinking about it. There were signs of past stubbornness, dirtiness, and inability to keep things together everywhere. Auri was more than happy to send those things where they belonged.

It is rarely the case that the resident is not at all disgusted by the condition into which his or her home has exploded. However, this is what people ask Auri, to the point of boredom. If the viewer of the video shudders, imagine how the person who lives there feels, Auri reminds. While she was cleaning a young couple's apartment, one of the parties was unable to visit the home's kitchen at all. The uncleanliness of it made her vomit. When she arrived home, she always headed straight to the couch, where she slept, ate, and spent all her time. Admittedly, most of the days she spent somewhere other than home, because it was too hard to be there.

Even while cleaning in the faraway UK, Auri got a tangible indication that people don't easily become blind to the chaos that surrounds them very easily. The woman, who had ventured out of an abusive relationship, had closed the door of her messy kitchen completely so she wouldn't have to see it.

## The Logic of Slippage

Although loneliness, if anything, drives people to indifference about their home, Auri has also seen other kinds of fates at cleaning gigs. Sometimes it is a loved one who takes someone with them into a crippling depression, where seemingly nothing matters. This happened to a girl who lived under the same roof as a severely depressed boy. The girl must have thought that love could heal him, make him cope better.

The girl had attached Post-it notes of different colors to the walls of their shared home, on which she had written detailed instructions for everyday life. They were full of prompts, such as *brush your teeth every night* and *put your phone away no later than ten o'clock in the evening*. But when you turned your gaze to the bathroom, there was a gigantic mountain of dishes in front of you. According to the girl, it had stood and molded in the shower for two years straight. So the girl's optimism was not enough.

The slippage aptly describes the mechanism that Auri has witnessed during cleaning gigs. In a way, like attracts like. It's a bit like dust attracting other dust balls to it; garbage is also screaming its invitation to another piece of rubbish. First, one measly piece of rubbish, bouncing harmlessly from one corner to the other, moving lightly on the floor. It can be a paper wrapper, a piece of foam that has flown out of a cardboard box, or a half-overturned soda bottle. The garbage rests quietly on the floor, and soon, as if out of pity for the lonely, its fellow garbage begins to gather around it.

The logic of dust and debris can also be said to apply to humans. If a person suffers from lack of money, food, or sleep, or has health problems, or all of them at the same time, they kind of invite mess to come to them. It is visible in almost every case, no matter how hard we try to convince ourselves it is easy to keep our homes clean and tidy.

Thus, Auri does not assume that the home she has cleaned will save a person's life like pushing a button. Auri does not assume that by polishing the sink or taking away the piles of rubbish, she will be able to fix the resident's gambling addiction or the chain of payment defaults. But it is possible, because just as an uncontrollable spiral starts with one problem, the same thread may be broken when one weight is lifted.

This is what happened to Erika, who is a couple years younger than Auri. The cleaning gig at her house is remembered for its special nature—partly because the home was, in Auri's language, one of the most wonderful. In other words, it was in terrible condition. Above all, it is because Auri has learned more about Erika's history and experiences after cleaning than she usually does from others who need her help.

Erika's story is also valuable because, after all the details and life experiences, you may forget what kind of people are hiding behind the messy homes shown in the videos. In most cases, there are ordinary people hiding there, whose ability to cope is compromised for one reason or another. People who would rather live in a cozy, normal-condition home than an exploded apartment. For many, a messy home is the most embarrassing and difficult thing in their life.

## Erika's Secret Nightmare

As a child, Erika was like everyone else. She wasn't passionate about keeping her room in order, and didn't volunteer to take out trash or scrub the kitchen. Her mother made sure that Erika was involved in the housework, and her room couldn't be turned into a landfill. The mother kept things spotless at home and told her daughter that the cleanliness of the home matters. From a young age, however, Erika had found it difficult to concentrate on things properly, both at home and at school. Erika progressed in life as expected, graduated from her secondary education, turned eighteen, and moved out.

Reality hit her in the face when she moved out on her own. Suddenly, no one came to start the vacuum cleaner, nor to take out the trash or to wash the dirty dishes multiplying in the sink. No one was holding Erika's hand, let alone making sure she was doing well. At first, her home remained tidy, but gradually, day by day, more and more, it began to resemble a mess that one could not cope with, or did not want to interfere with. Since Erika didn't know anyone from her new hometown, she didn't have any friends to invite to visit, so the mess never had to be hidden from anyone.

Loneliness triggered mental health problems that had been raging beneath the surface for a long time. Erika suffered from depression and became suicidal, fueled by the aching memory of being a rape victim. Erika told Auri it had been difficult to believe that good things could happen to her. Instead, Erika said she only sees evil in front of her. It had happened before, so it was expected to happen again.

Instead of being trapped in one apartment, Erika had moved to many different addresses and changed cities. In every move, she had followed the same method: the floor could be cleared by stuffing everything in a garbage bag and taking it to the trash. There was no need to go through the stuff, let alone rearrange it, as the mess followed like a ghost from one apartment to another. At first it remained hidden in the cupboards, until it was allowed to crawl out into the apartment again.

*Erika's disgust for the disorganization of the apartment was directly connected with shame.*

Erika never turned a blind eye to the chaos. The mess wasn't made by accident or stealth, but because she just couldn't intervene. And every time the mess arrived, it felt just as bad and humiliating. She hated her home every damn morning, day, evening, and night. Erika's disgust for the disorganization of the apartment was directly connected with shame.

"Why can't I do something about it? Why doesn't my home look the same as other people's homes?" Erika scolded herself for being messy, day in and day out.

Then, when she tried to cheer up, collect the garbage in a bag, the situation was interrupted by a panic attack. She was frustrated and infuriated that an ordinary household chore could produce so much pain and repulsion. The mere act of forcing herself to take out the trash sometimes made her feel physically unwell.

*You can't let anyone in here and you can't tell anyone about this. This is neither normal nor acceptable, and no one gets to see what condition I have gotten my home in,* Erika told herself.

Although Erika later found friends and received support from them for her problems, she never let them into her home. Even those whom Erika had openly told that she suffered from serious mental health problems and went to therapy were not invited to visit. She spent time with her friends in other people's homes, having coffee, or going out to the city. She studied at a university, went to work regularly, and met people without them ever being able to guess what condition her home was in. She furthered the illusion by making herself look as well-groomed and tidy as possible, whenever she escaped from the oppressive landfill to be in front of people. Even Erika's longtime psychologist had no clue that her home was not in a habitable condition. Although Erika was and still is able to express her darkest feelings and most painful traumas in therapy, the shame of having a messy home was too much. She didn't dare to admit it. Her messy home had become, in Erika's words, a secret nightmare in which no one else had a part. Why was the condition of the home more shameful than, say, having deliberately hurt oneself? Neither Erika nor Auri can say for sure. Perhaps it is that keeping the home in good condition is still taken for granted in the public and in society. Just an everyday routine that needs to be accomplished, whatever the situation. After all, home is the nesting place where we spend the most time. And cleaning isn't reading the laws of physics or deep-sea diving, but something that should go smoothly, even for a normal person.

Her messy home had become, in Erika's words, a secret nightmare in which no one else had a part.

Erika's case was also more interesting because she was not blind to the reception of Auri's videos, for example. When Auri cleans up, doubts may appear in the comments about whether a person who uses drugs or is otherwise dubious lives in the home. The amount of people who had fallen off the course of society and stayed there haunted Erika.

"Yes, I secretly envied my friends and mom's home when they're so clean. *Why don't I have that, why can't I do it, why do I just mess up all the time?* Even then, I felt like something was wrong with me," Erika said, and continued, "Individual comments say yes, some junkie or drunk lives there. I'm neither, and even if I were, that's not a reason to shame anyone.

"People have different problems, and it is often not a matter of laziness or indifference. For example, if I had been able to choose, I would never have lived in a home that was in such terrible condition. But I had the feeling that I couldn't live anymore, no one needed me. I didn't even need myself because I hated myself so much.

"I would like to see more humanity. I've even looked at a picture of a messy apartment in the past and called it a dump, and I regret it.

Now I am tempted to say, 'God give them mercy.' I would also like to say that you can't necessarily know what your friends or relatives are going through. Maybe that's why I urge you to ask your friends if they're okay.

"They are not always okay. Even a simple question can often make it easier. It's enough to be present and listen."

*You can't necessarily know what your friends or relatives are going through.*

When Erika finally dared to contact Auri, she responded to the email right away. In her message, Erika had thanked Auri for the work she had done for others. "I feel so good when I see your updates," Erika had written. After that, she was open about her situation: depression took away her strength to clean up, but now she felt better and didn't feel like dying every day. The message began and ended with a red heart, accompanied by pictures of the condition of the apartment.

Auri knew right away that she would like to go and help Erika as quickly as she could. Soon they agreed that Auri would come and clean the very next day.

When Auri opened the door of Erika's home, she discovered that the rubbish had actually taken over all the surface areas of the apartment.

As in many other locations, the shower and balcony were covered with debris and mountains of trash. Erika's bed, too, was buried, an unrecognizable pile, under the garbage. Auri couldn't imagine how Erika had even been able to sleep.

The fact that the bed was covered in rubbish was no more shocking for Erika than the messiness of the apartment otherwise. Auri remembers Erika saying "If you feel like you are one with the garbage, it is natural to surround yourself with it." The phrase has stayed in Auri's mind afterwards. When you don't value yourself, you may no longer feel the need to keep your home in order. And when a home becomes a disaster hotspot, it can become an important and essential reminder of one's own inadequacy and inferiority.

Auri cleaned Erika's home as usual for two days. When Erika returned to her apartment, she burst into tears. Erika saw the floor, her lovely floor, for the first time in several months.

But even though the apartment was clean again, the shame of the home mysteriously did not disappear. Erika had promised Auri in advance that the apartment could be filmed for video. Now she was scared that someone would recognize the apartment from the video. Would the dump be associated with her? What would her friends say? What would everyone think?

Auri vowed that this would not happen, as all the details about Erika would be erased. This turned out to be true, and Erika was able to continue her life as usual. The difference was that she could stay at home normally, without worrying that walls of stuff and rubbish would fall over. When she got tired in the evenings, she could fall on the bed on nothing but the sheets. Colorful plastic wrappers and packets did not creak under the blanket, and the soles of her feet did not collide with empty bottles or cans.

## Common to All of Us

Erika's biggest fear was that someone she knew would recognize the apartment as her home in the video. Her fear was not exceptional, but an indication of the value we attach to the home. If the home is not tidy and orderly, we are afraid that we will be labeled an unworthy person.

Therefore, it is out of the question for Auri to expect people who receive cleaning to appear in the videos with their own names and faces. It would be completely pointless for Auri, and would take attention away from what matters to her and to the viewers of the videos—namely, that it is possible to clean and turn a home which has reached a frenzied condition into a cozy one again. That's the most important message Auri wants to convey with her videos.

Although Auri loves, really loves, cleaning and its outcome, she does not go to homes to incite shame because of what caused the situation. Rather, the videos are a sign that chaos can get the upper hand over anyone. A messy apartment is not a shocking exception from the other side of the globe, but a normal everyday sight for Auri. And hey: without the mess, there wouldn't be anything for her to clean.

Thus, the video captured from the cleaning gig does not humiliate the person living there. It doesn't put them in an embarrassing light. The point is only to prove that every apartment can be cleaned. It doesn't matter if the dirt and clutter has been brewing on the property for weeks, months, or years. The fact that various tragedies are actually hidden behind the videos also indicates that the home is not a reflection of their weakness.

The principle that Auri sticks to at cleaning gigs is unequivocal: she does not advise cleaning correctly or better. She believes that people know how to clean, but for various reasons have not been able or willing to do so. Cleaning gigs are acts of charity and an opportunity for the resident to have a fresh start. What happens after the cleaning is up to the resident.

And while there may be more tragic stories in the background, a cleaning gig is first and foremost a joyful gig. You don't go there crying or groaning. You go there to enjoy the process. Perhaps that distinguishes Auri from what we usually hear in stories. Katriina Järvinen, a psychotherapist whom I recently interviewed on a completely different topic, thinks so. Unsolicited and unexpectedly, she brought up Auri, who, in Katriina's opinion, is doing God's work.

Katriina said that Auri cranks up the shame we are used to, from which cleaning stress partly stems, in a new way. I think that was rightly said. In Auri's world, mess and dirt have nothing to do with dignity, morality, or shame.

Dirty homes are cleaned up to make them feel good. Entering an apartment resembling a landfill does not mean the screams of pain and heart-pounding tense music typical of American dramas, but rather, therapeutic action with an affirmational undertone.

So shame is by far the worst and most pernicious motivator for cleaning. It's a slowdown, or an outright obstacle, to liking cleaning. But when you get past it, like Auri, you might fall head over heels in love with cleaning.

# CHAPTER 5

# PRECISION *Tips*

## The Holy Trinity of Cleaning

1.  *Detergent.* What detergent does the cleaner use? Acidic, alkaline, or neutral? And is the substance in sprayable or spreadable form?

2.  *Time.* Is the cleaner in a hurry, or do they have plenty of time? Can a cleaner work for hours, or even overnight? Or does it need to be rinsed suddenly?

3.  *Mechanics* (i.e. the instrument in use and how hard you rub with it). What kind of mechanics are used? How hard does the cleaner have to help, and how hard can they rub the surfaces with it? Is it worth choosing an effective,

popular cleaning blade, or does a microfiber towel beat everything else?

The holy trinity of cleaning is the most solid cornerstone for Auri and many other professional cleaners. The final result is determined by these three elements. The trick of the Trinity lies in the fact that the cleaning process can be influenced by changing the focus between members of the trio.

For example, if a cleaner only has a little bit of time at his disposal, it is worth investing in an effective tool and substances. If, on the other hand, the active detergent is allowed to remain in the pot for a long time, the mechanics may not be needed at all. Auri encourages you to think about which part of the Trinity to invest in this time and what to skip.

Auri remembers how the triad commonly used in the cleaning industry revolutionized her own cleaning ideology a few years ago. She was cleaning the oven of her then-boyfriend, Sami, which had been seriously burned and was therefore very difficult to clean. Although the burnt spots were aggressively scraped off, there was no way they would disappear from the oven walls. Soon Auri got tired of the scrubbing and fell into her thoughts for a moment.

Suddenly, a thought occurred to her: This must have taken some time. In retrospect, the solution is downright self-evident to Auri, but at the time the idea was revolutionary. To leave the detergent in action and go elsewhere, not to try and beat it with muscle strength? It was then that Auri imagined a stubborn, dried slice of cucumber stuck on the floor in front of her. It doesn't come

off right away either, no matter how much you scrub and scrape. But if you keep cool and drop water on top of the slice, it will soften in a few minutes so that you can just pick it up and drop it into the biowaste.

Cleaning the oven was made challenging by the fact that the wall is vertical. How can you make the detergent stay on it long enough? With plastic wrap, Auri answered her own question, as if the answer was in the subconscious just waiting for permission to come forward. Soon she lined the oven with cling film and oven cleaner, closed the door, and waited patiently for many hours.

And, hallelujah, it paid off! When the cling film came out of the oven, the dirt had indeed melted beneath it. This made Auri triumphant.

Little by little, with her success, she began to believe that she could not encounter dirt that she would not overcome by experimenting with different methods.

With three contributing factors, strategy has remained a permanent part of Auri's cleaning. In particular, she emphasizes the importance of time, which is missed in many households. If there is a coffee mark in the sink, it will not come off, even if chlorine bleach is sprinkled on top of it. Chlorine bleach must always be allowed to sit for a few minutes so that things start to happen. And when food is stuck on a surface, just pouring water on it allows her to wait for the end result.

The effect of time also emerges in the hectic everyday life of professional cleaners. Auri takes as an example washing the walls, floors, and faucets of the shower. It is a physically strenuous task for the cleaner: it involves reaching from the heights down to the floor, moving from top to bottom.

If the boss of cleaning professionals doesn't want to break the backs of their cleaners, it is smart to reduce mechanical abrasion and add plenty of detergent and time.

"In other words, you spread a lot of detergent, apply the solution to the wall, and let it be," Auri sums up. And only when the substance has had time to cast its spell without a human hand will the shower shine again.

At a cleaning gig, Auri and I are confronted by a nightmarish-looking toilet bowl. It is so brown that one might think that it should be brown and not white. I don't know if it has ever seen a toilet brush. Auri says right away that the only thing that can save this is detergent that needs to be given a lot of time. Having discovered this, she pours a strong, professionally traded bluish acid into the bowl, which, however, consists mostly of vinegar. Then Auri closes the lid and says, let's bulldoze some more tomorrow.

When we return to the apartment in the morning, light mechanics are enough to scrape off the remaining brown. The acid has done its job. An unidentifiable toilet bowl turned into a real toilet bowl, the porcelain of which glows white. Patience paid off. The holy trinity works with any emphasis, and none of them should be overlooked, especially not mechanics. Sometimes just a hard tool and a powerful pair of hands are enough to remove dirt. In this case, cleaning products that smell strong can be left in the back of the cleaning cabinet or, even better, in the store. According to Auri, however, we are most keen on cleaning products.

While jars are eagerly hauled from the store in plastic bags, there is almost a fear of proper equipment and its supposedly destructive effect. In the midst of a buying frenzy, it is also often not considered that the detergent must have time to act. Not to mention the fact that the detergent may not be needed at all.

Although Auri doesn't profess to be an eco-cleaner or just a water-slapper, her thesis is unequivocal: A little goes a long way. Sometimes just dishwashing liquid is enough.

## The Secret Substance for the Sink

If you ask Auri, the cleaning product market is a wild and unreasonable zone. The consumer comes across more and more extraordinary substances, one designed against the smells of the refrigerator, the second for rancid stench, the third for other surfaces in the bathroom, the fourth for an exploded food mess in the microwave, and the fifth for grimy balcony chairs. However, the vast majority of products contain a similar mild all-purpose cleaner. So, for the most part, they consist of water mixed with a small amount of cleaning agent.

For example, if a substance promises to expel odors as it goes, like many bathroom sprays, there is probably a drop of acid in it, as bacteria do not live in an acidic environment, but are destroyed by it. A substance classified as suitable for the bathroom is not bad

or unworthy, but it should not be treated as a more miraculous invention than, for example, dishwashing liquid.

According to Auri, the thing that the market is silent about, as if it were an unspoken agreement, is precisely the power of the detergent in dishwashing liquid. Yes, it's all about that beautifully foaming Fairy or similar product that is sold solely for cleaning dirty dishes.

However, professional cleaners have always known the secret of dishwashing detergents. Whether you're faced with stained drawers in the kitchen, walls hit with leftovers from dinner, or a sink full of soap residue, the first thing is often the same: hand dishwashing liquid, water, and a soft sponge, and you can get going. Bomb apartments do not require different marching orders either, since familiar and safe dishwashing soap can produce astounding results there as well.

The infallibility of the dishwashing detergent lies in the fact that it is a fairly neutral substance that you can try for almost anything. It works especially on greasy dirt, such as soap residue, because it is itself a stronger substance than soap, i.e. a substance with a more alkaline pH value.

Sometimes, if Auri needs to spray something like the inside of a refrigerator, she fills a spray bottle with warm water and mixes it with a splash of dishwashing liquid. When the substance is sprayed, it conveniently spreads over a wide area. However, the spray bottle has its problems. Firstly, sprayable substances may not be as effective as solids, and secondly, when sprayed, chemicals also float into the room air. If you use sprays a lot and thus inhale them all the time, they can cause allergy or other irritation symptoms.

Because of this, professional cleaners do not spray cleaning products with spray bottles away from home. Auri herself has not been allergic to cleaning products over the years, but she understands that many people become sensitive to them after even minimal use. Fortunately, there are plenty of options.

> ### TIME AND MUSCLE STRENGTH SAVING TIP: EVERYTHING TO THE MACHINE!
>
> Do not forget about the dishwasher! The dishwasher is very likely to be filled with just dishes, as the name predicts. You can throw a lot more into the machine for a short wash cycle. For example, try washing the baking trays that have been messed up by burnt food, the grease filters in the hood, the glass plate from the microwave, the strainer in the sink, the oven racks, the loose parts of the coffee maker and the air fryer, and the refrigerator shelves. For example, small trash cans and parts of a barbecue in the yard are equally suitable there. You might be surprised at how clean they all become.

### If Nothing Else Helps

What should I do if dishwashing detergent doesn't help? That can happen sometimes. For Auri, who cleans uninhabitable homes, dishwashing detergent is first and foremost first aid. If it doesn't work, Auri grabs the heavier weapons. At our joint cleaning gig, this weapon is oven cleaner. Auri applies it after the dishwashing liquid to the ceramic hob and the transparent glass of the hood, both of which are covered with stubborn grease. At the same time, the sponge is replaced by a Steel Scour Daddy.

It is not worth trying oven cleaner without gloves that protect your hands. Auri doesn't recommend it except as a last resort (but a very effective one). If you decide to test the oven cleaner at home, be careful with it. The substance may cause damage, for example, to a wooden floor. Auri learned this the hard way when she was in Sami's backyard, washing the grill with an oven cleaner. Suddenly, it accidentally fell to the ground. Only a moment passed, but a noticeable amount of color came off the wooden patio floor.

In addition to wood, oven cleaner may also cause stains on other surfaces. Although, in principle, it should not damage a painted wall, Auri still would not smear the walls with an oven cleaner. She uses it only and exclusively on hard surfaces, because she knows that it works as it should.

The least compatible partner for oven cleaner is probably aluminum, with which the oven cleaner can create a combustion reaction. Some may have tried Auri's cling film method by replacing the cling film with aluminum foil, which has set the oven on fire. In other words: do not combine foil with oven cleaner!

In any case, no matter what you think of oven cleaner, it's mind-boggling to see how it starts to corrode dirt away, as if by itself. It shows me how an effective substance makes what seems impossible possible. The application of the substance is followed by the trajectory performed by Auri with a cleaning cloth. The towel runs from corner to corner and leaves no trace of loose dirt, just a flat glossy surface. You could stare at her cleaning for hours without getting bored.

## Two Types of Dirt

When you're looking for a suitable cleaning agent, you should always have in mind something besides the detergent, or even which room you are working in. The gaze must be focused on the dirt itself and its composition. The choice of substance is indicated by whether the dirt is shiny grease, or more crystal-like limescale. Of the two, limescale is the more stubborn one. If water stands still, for example in the kitchen or in the bathroom, then most likely limescale will lurk there, and not grease dirt. However, even grease can sometimes look the same when, for example, grease balls dry on the tiles located behind the stove.

However, while grease is soft, limescale is hard. This is Auri's way of roughly dividing dirt into two groups. Soft means sticky and leathery dirt that typically finds its way into the kitchen sink or bathroom sink. Soft dirt can be recognized by the fact that when you touch the sink with your finger, it feels sticky. *Ii-ii*, Auri imitates the sound emanating from a greasy sink. Fat is released from human skin (oil) and from soap, for example. An alkaline substance, such as chlorine, oven cleaner, or dishwashing detergent, is applied to soft dirt. If, on the other hand, the sink feels dry or hard, it literally has hard dirt, such as limescale or rust. For hard dirt, not an alkaline but an acidic substance—such as vinegar—is effective. The detergents used in the toilet are especially acidic. In other words, typical toilet detergents do

remove hard dirt and stench smoothly, but in the face of grease dirt that accumulates in the bathroom, they are powerless.

It is important not to mix acidic and alkaline substances together, even if at some point one needs them both. Especially, strong acid and chlorine form a toxic gas in combination that you should not play with. If you want to clean bathroom surfaces with both acid and alkali, you need to rinse the surfaces thoroughly between treatments. In addition to the potential toxicity, the efficacy of acid and alkali is lost if they mix.

An apt example of a collector of two different types of dirt is a coffee machine, a gadget that dispenses salvation to sleep-deprived people in numerous Finnish homes. The passage of coffee through the machinery spreads grease dirt there, but at the same time, the stagnant water makes the pot a chalky mess of limescale. Many people clean their coffee machines with a cleaning tablet sold in supermarkets and designed for the machine's kettle (water heater) itself.

We don't necessarily check whether the tablet is alkaline or acidic (there are both sorts of them on the market), let alone whether the coffee maker needs alkaline, acidic, or both. With a very high probability and Auri's experience, it will scream both.

Therefore, Auri first dispenses into the kettle, in the water, either a degreaser or an alkaline coffee machine cleaner tablet. Then she clicks the machine on and stops the program in the middle. The mixture is allowed to swim in the depths of the machine for a quarter or half-hour, until extensive rinsing begins. Full pans can be rinsed five times so that the acidic and alkaline do not mix together. If that happens, the result will be a big zero, as they cancel each other out.

After rinsing, Auri pours plenty of vinegar into the kettle, in the water, and again interrupts the program in the middle. Even vinegar is allowed to stay in the kettle for half an hour, until the merciless rinsing operation begins again. Finally, the outer surfaces of the machine can still be brushed with a dish brush and dishwashing liquid.

In principle, greasy dirt works equally with chlorine. Auri also knows the trick of instructing the coffee machine to clean, with the power of a dishwashing tablet. The trick may well work, but Auri hasn't tried it. However, if you want to try, you should rinse the coffee maker many times.

## LET'S RECAP: HOW MANY SUBSTANCES DOES A HOME CLEANER GO A LONG WAY WITH?

The answer is four.

1. **Dishwashing detergent.** A cleaner's assistant that you should boldly try on almost any dirt.

2. **Acidic substance.** If the pH value is less than seven, the substance can be defined as acidic. One example of an acidic substance is vinegar. It works on hard dirt, such as limescale.

3. **Alkaline substance.** In turn, if the pH value is more than seven, the substance can be defined as alkaline. Strongly alkaline substances include, for example, chlorine and oven cleaner. The base (alkali) works on soft grease dirt.

4. **Cleaning stone.** You may remember how that very stone saved the author's job at the end of the summer. The Stone of Purification is like an unknown hero who deserves even more kudos on Auri's behalf.

   The cleaning stone crowns the end result with its polishing (and even surprising) effect. It is suitable for almost all surfaces in the home, and is made of organic clay. If nothing else works, the cleaning stone might be a surprising path to happiness and bliss.

# A Word About Mechanics and Smiling Sponges

In recent years, cleaning has also started to talk about ecology.

Will cleaning products destroy the earth? Auri cannot call herself an eco-cleaner, as she has to use strong substances at cleaning gigs in exceptionally stubborn places. Despite this, she belongs to the camp that calls for fewer cleaning products. Based on Auri's experience, mechanics beat substances.

According to Auri, a home whose residents clean (at least quite) regularly survives with mild, environmentally friendly substances, the four listed in the previous paragraph. That is, dishwashing detergent, one acidic and one alkaline substance, plus a cleaning stone. In the best-case scenario, substances can sometimes be pushed aside completely and we can rely

on seamless cooperation between water and mechanics. Many people underestimate the importance of mechanics in cleaning. When followers ask Auri for tips, they're more interested in the cleanser than anything. What cleanser did you have in that video? And what substance would you use for this?

If, for example, limescale grows on the floor, and Auri removes it with a cleaning blade, water, and a splash of vinegar, then 99 percent of people are only interested in the vinegar. In the hands of Auri or many other professional cleaners, a sponge, prone to odors and unhygienic, will not be worth bothering with. In Auri's opinion, it will end up in the dustbin of cleaning equipment.

However, there was a significant crack in Auri's years-long sponge hatred recently. Her current main sponsor, Scrub Daddy, which makes smiling and colorful sponges, had contacted her in the wake of dozens, if not hundreds, of other cleaning companies.

What was special was that Auri had, just before they contacted her, gotten her hands o a product from the same manufacturer in the supermarket. She was determined to see if there was any truth to the fuss, from the invention presented in the Lion's Den series.

Skepticism suddenly melted into astonishment, and soon she fell in love. The trick of this sponge lies in its large surface area, durability, and deformability: under warm water, the sponge softens, and in cold, it hardens.

Whereas in the past Auri used to apply detergent to surfaces with the help of a dish brush, today she performs the rite with a sponge soaked with warm water. The sponge absorbs the substance properly, and due to its large size, it also spreads the substance widely. And when the surface is rinsed and wiped, the dirt disappears with the sponge. Auri washes sponges and dish brushes with the hottest program in the dishwasher, at 70 degrees Celsius (158 Fahrenheit), so that the bacteria are guaranteed to die.

Auri cannot name a single place where such a soft sponge wouldn't do a lot of good. It is no exaggeration to say that she uses it everywhere. It's easy to teach children to clean the shower room during the Saturday sauna, when the sponge is a cute toy in their hands. Auri would like to spread that attitude to adults as well. If the cleaning equipment is nice, could cleaning be a bit like playing? Could it be an opportunity to surrender to a chore that makes you feel relaxed and takes you back to childhood for a while?

## Ode to Scraper

If truth be told, many of us are afraid of, and even shy away, from scrubbing the surfaces of our homes. We have bad dreams about scratches and imagine that the home can be shattered by the power of mere thought. Auri isn't worried about this scenario after years of mechanics-driven cleaning.

This is evidenced by the way she works at cleaning gigs. First, Auri starts with a cleaning sponge. If a traditional sponge is too soft, a scrubbing sponge containing steel—or, most confusingly, a relatively small cleaning blade about six centimeters (two inches) long—will leap to her hand from the range of equipment. Auri calls the sharp-angled, plastic-framed blade by the nickname "skrapa."

According to Auri, along with dishwashing detergent and the microfiber towel, the cleaning blade is the best friend of professional cleaners. You can understand that when you and Auri are cleaning a bomb apartment. For Auri, utilizing the blade in cleaning is an important part of the project.

If, for example, the stains attached to the dining table can't be removed, a cleaning blade will come and scrape them out of sight in a couple of seconds at Auri's fingertips. The same applies to a number of other points, which are sometimes surprising. Dirt stuck inside of the oven, or in the glass of the oven door. Stains on the upper part of the hood and on the back wall of the stove. Paint stuck to the window. Burnt food in a saucepan. Food traces in kitchen cabinets, inside and out. And limescale, of course, limescale, wherever it is.

"Everything burnt and hardened is skrapa's business. It beats all the others," Auri emphasizes. In other words, window cleaning, for example, is often synonymous with water and light scratching for Auri. Everything has to go, however, whether it's stains, dust, or both. On the other hand, Auri knows of a case where a cleaning company managed to get the windows of twenty-six apartment buildings scratched with just such a cleaning blade. So you must use caution, at least when cleaning the most delicate surfaces.

A good way to ensure the safety of scraping is to first try it only on a small, invisible area.

The cleaning blade can be used with water alone, but also with dishwashing liquid or even oven cleaner mixed with water. Combining it with the detergent makes the surface slippery and makes the work smoother. So it takes less time. In the case of stubborn, stubborn stubbornness, even the most effective substance rarely achieves anything unless you try rubbing with it.

Many people may apply vinegar, or more special substances, to the stains. The movement is at least as important as the substance. A person may sometimes notice that a pretty bunch of banknotes has been spent on cleaning products, but they have not worked that well. At the same time, just a tiny skrapa and its scratching motion would have removed the rancid yellow, or grayed-out, dirt spots in no time. Nonsense? If you try it, you might be surprised.

Auri is pleased that, especially when cleaning an induction stove, people dare to use force.

She encourages the same enthusiasm elsewhere, such as at the tap in the toilet. Over time, yellow dirt is deposited around the sink, which many people agonize over. Auri remembers how she herself used to be able to use and smear various acids and leave them on surfaces to work—to no avail. If she could now time-travel to the past, she would take the more inexperienced

Auri by the hand and direct her to scramble through all the glory. Although an induction stove can be cleaned with a blade, a ceramic stove with elevated hobs in many households is a more challenging case. What can you do about its dirt deposits? Auri suggests a peculiar-sounding solution: spray oven cleaner on the surface and put on the plastic wrap familiar from Sami's oven. After that, let's play with time. Only time thaws away the dirt, so you can leave the cling film on the entire stove for one night. In the morning, a nice sight awaits the person trying the trick. If individual burnt dirt remains, it can be removed with a cleaning blade or a steel scouring sponge.

## Rag Is a Swear Word

Steel cleaning equipment is strong, but Auri also prefers more peaceful tools in everyday life. For example, the dish brush is a real luxury invention for her. Like dishwashing detergent, the dish brush is also suitable for uses other than those described in the name.

The brush-like tool allows you to slip into small crevices, and especially when cleaning toilets and kitchen sinks, it is an unfailing choice. The dish brush removes dirt from small spaces, and may open a clogged sink when it is used to clean the screen. But because the dish brush is soft, it does not remove stubborn stains, and is as effective as a soft sponge.

After removing the dirt with the dish brush, you can naturally grab a microfiber towel. It is almost an adored tool in cleaning circles, which is not a conventional towel but perhaps the most important tool for a cleaner, because it's used every single time. Whether Auri is cleaning a bomb home or her own home, she invariably digs it up. Perhaps the worst mistake Auri knows is to call the towel a rag. It's by no means a rag, Auri exclaims.

"A rag reminds me of something dirty, smelly, broken, and disgusting. When I was working my day job, I deliberately tried to teach the cleaners not to call cloths or towels rags. Although it is just a word, the way we speak has an impact on how we relate to a job. The same applies, by the way, to the lute, which is also a name far from promising or attractive."

The microfiber towel works for daily table wiping, dusting, and more demanding uses.

The most surprising example is the dark spots nestled on the ceiling of the bathroom, which Auri encourages us to try to clean with a microfiber towel and water. Spots often indicate moisture that cannot be avoided in bathrooms. However, the towel does not remove mold from the silicone caulk seams, as the mold never leaves the silicone. In this case, the only way to get the seams clean is to completely replace their silicone parts with new ones. In order for the microfiber towel to work as it should, it is worth remembering at least two things.

First of all: The towel must definitely be clean.

So it is not suitable to throw the dirty towel in the closet. The action of the towel is based on the fact that it collects dust and dirt on itself from the surface.

When you start wiping again with a microfiber towel, and it starts to hand over the dirt it has collected again, the towel is either not washed at all, or it has been cleaned carelessly. The most abominable (and by far the worst!) way is to rinse the towel in the bucket, twist it dry, and continue on the same track. If the intention is to clean the entire apartment, it is not at all foolish to reserve several microfiber towels for the cleaning so that there is enough clean wiping surface. So-called color coding, i.e., using towels of different colors in the toilet and in the kitchen, is also a practical trick. After use, Auri washes the towels in the washing machine at a high setting, i.e. 90 degrees (194 F), not 60 degrees (140 F), where many people wash their cleaning textiles. Based on Auri's experience, such a low heat reading is not always enough, and on the other hand, microfiber towels can withstand even hotter temperatures. In a hot enough wash program, all bacteria die, so it doesn't matter if you wipe the insides of the toilet or the dining table after that.

Since the microfiber towel consists of open fibers, it collects dust around it. Therefore, these towels should be washed separately from other textiles, such as clothes, sheets, and regular towels.

On the absolute ban list, Auri places fabric softener that many, such as Auri's editor and translator Nea in the past, have poured into the machine in the hope of a fresh scent. Nea then agonized to Auri that the towels weren't working as they should. The harmless-looking softener was guaranteed to clog the fibers of the towel, and thus it can no longer collect dirt inside.

You shouldn't mash a microfiber towel into a mess and then go without a head, tail, sense, and rules. The trick is in the versatile surface of the towel. It can be divided into up to eight parts by folding. Many professional cleaners tend to divide it into only four, but Auri leans toward double the amount so that there are enough surfaces that there is no need to change the equipment all the time.

Each part is used at a time for a while, and then switched to the clean side. By folding the towel, you get eight times the amount of clean surface on it, which feels revolutionary. Auri assures that, when you learn the most competent folding technique meticulously, it will start to work out. The most typical mistake for a beginner is that, instead of whole sections, they fold the towel in half. It's like wiping with a dumpling that just spreads dirt around it.

At first, the folding operation can make some heads spin, there is no denying it. But then, one day, the folding begins to go smoothly and by reflex. This has happened to all the cleaners trained by Auri, and Auri believes that it will happen to anyone who has the patience to learn the technique. At first, it is enough to be aware that a microfiber towel has at best eight small towels inside it, and not just two sides that get dirty in an instant.

Also, in the light of studies, a microfiber towel is incomparable as a cleaning tool. It has been proven that such a towel and water remove 99 percent of bacteria and dirt when used correctly. One study that emerged from Auri's work, on the other hand, wanted to find out whether a hospital room became cleaner the longer the cleaner operated there with towels.

It turned out that the second-fastest-cleaned room was the cleanest. In turn, the slowest cleaners got the worst results.

This shows that time use rarely correlates with how clean something gets. It is essential that the technology, such as the way the microfiber towel is folded, is in the loop. More importantly, the microfiber towel has been used in the first place.

Auri has actually raised the use of the towel to its own heights. She has replaced vacuuming, the king of everyday chores in Finnish homes, with a strategy in which the microfiber towel plays the second main role.

So how do you actually fold that towel?

Moisten a towel, then twist and squeeze it so that no more water drips from it. The more water you can wring out, the better. Then open the towel completely and fold in half. Fold again. In your hands should be a square, a quarter of a towel. Fold the towel one more time. Now the towel is folded three times, and in your hands is the appropriate package.

Start with the first surface. When it is dirty, fold a new side of the towel so that the inside is open. Now you have a perfectly clean surface in your hand again, and you can move on to wiping a new spot.

When the time comes again to change the surface, the towel should be opened in half and half. In other words: open the towel lengthwise, and then use the other side in the same way. After that, there is still the other side of the towel completely unused, which will be used as well. With this method, you can wipe several different surfaces with one towel. It speeds up wiping and makes it more hygienic.

The most common mistake in folding is not making enough good folds. Thus, dirt can easily get into other layers as well, and folding does not bring the greatest benefit. Another mistake is often that the towel is too wet, causing it to give up water and spread dirt.

Folding a towel is, above all, a sport that you learn by practicing.

"I just decided that I was going to start folding. It didn't work out at all at first, but little by little it got into a groove. Today it's like it's automatic," Auri says.

## Vacuuming a Waste of Time? Yep!

When Auri revealed to reporters, including myself, that she thought vacuuming was pointless, people shrugged. Some snorted, others were inspired. In the aftermath of her proclamation, Auri was met with a great deal of wonder and criticism. How did a cleaning guru dare to claim that a vacuum cleaner is not needed in her everyday life? After all, it takes the longest time in a weekly cleaning. Auri stands behind her claim with confidence. She does not get tired of emphasizing the fact that the harmony of cleaning at home does not need to be interrupted by the roar of the vacuum cleaner. When the vacuum cleaner starts buzzing, its sound really takes over the whole house, and often swings the cleaner's stress levels upward in an instant. Could the solution to the cleaning frenzy be Auri's rather provocative claim that wiping can do just as much, or actually more—and even faster? For Auri, vacuuming has for years meant a heavy, annoying back-and-forth from corner to corner. At the same time, the device raises dust into the air, toward the surfaces of the home, so that after vacuuming, the air in the room does not feel fresher in the nose than before it. Auri has moved the vacuum cleaner to the back of the cabinet, as its cord only needs to be rolled open in exceptional cases.

The same thing happened with the robot vacuum of best friend Anni and her husband Lauri; it has been allowed to owl in the

closet for a year now, abandoned. While the cleaning method taught by the cleaning guru takes only ten minutes, Anni and Lauri's vacuum cleaner would spin on the job for three hours. But it's not spinning anymore.

Instead of the vacuum, Auri and Anni use a squeegee. The trick is to slip, yes, a damp microfiber towel onto it. Then the squeegee is used to go over the floors in the apartment. It doesn't take many minutes for the home to be clean on all its surfaces. Also, during the cleaning gig of an apartment in an uninhabitable condition, I noticed how effective the method is. Even if the floor is filled with tiny bits of debris and clumps of dirt, the microfiber towel really absorbs them.

However, the squeegee must be decent. Auri's spouse Sami remembers well the time when he and Auri were just dating. Already, at that time, Auri's eyes had been hit by an inferior bathroom drying spatula (squeegee) in his apartment, which upset her. Despite the insinuations, Sami did not invest in a new instrument, a decent squeegee, which, to Auri's mind, belongs in the same league as the tiny cleaning blade. Once, when Auri was staying with Sami for the night and Sami was asleep, Auri stared at the drying spatula in disgust and hurried to the store to buy a proper one. When Sami woke up, he found a video on his phone in which Auri had jumped on the drying spatula and dramatically shoved it into a trash can.

The power of the squeegee dryer is based on the working width. The nozzle of the vacuum cleaner has half the area of the squeegee blade, so the dryer simply extends wider. Since the vacuum cleaner does not wipe but puffs up and, as it were, tramples dirt more tightly to the floor, vacuuming is often followed by a separate chore: wiping the floors with a mop or similar cleaning tool. In everyday language, chores are also referred to as washing, but professional cleaners do not say that they wash floors, because for them it means that it would be soaked with water. In Auri's opinion, the method combining vacuuming and wiping floors is painfully laborious, and takes time away from more intense cleaning tasks.

If you decide to replace the vacuum cleaner with a squeegee, folding the microfiber towel is once again everything. First, one side is used, then one switches to the other. Because of this, cleaning floors with a folded microfiber towel is better than mopping, for example. The mop operates all the time on the same ropy, dreadlocks-like surface, which does not clean very well, even if it is rinsed in a bucket between washes.

Instead of going to all corners with the dryer, she mainly cleans the kitchen floor and the hallways in her home. The end result looks and feels the same as after vacuuming the house for an hour or two.

Is it then worth hurrying the vacuum to the recycling center to save space in the cleaning cupboard? No, and Auri has not done so and does not intend to do so. Even though the vacuum does not often do much work at home, it sometimes does anyway. In the midst of removing crumbs from boxes or cleaning carpets, for example.

In fact, when cleaning carpets, Auri swears by vacuuming or brushing, not the old folk trick, i.e. tamping. Tamping is old-fashioned for her, as it statically electrifies the carpet, and the dirt goes deeper. The vacuum cleaner is also suitable for cleaning textile furniture, such as sofas and bed frames. However, even in this matter, Auri prefers variety. Sometimes she uses a vacuum cleaner, sometimes she uses a textile washer, and on some cleaning days, she digs a wild card out of naphthalene: a window squeegee or a dish brush. When the rug or sofa surfaces are brushed with a dish brush removed from its original use, dirt and dust suddenly come off it.

And if you don't want to give up weekly vacuuming, Auri advises letting go of one bad habit. That is vacuuming on too high power. Many people set the vacuum cleaner right on high and let it pant heavily throughout the operation. What if, next time you vacuumed, you set it at first or second power and noticed how smoothly you moved forward? At the same time, you may notice that dirt does not leave more slowly or harder, even if the vacuum cleaner is not at full power. It may be the other way around, that dirt no longer sticks to the floor under an aggressive, screaming, and blowing device. It could delight especially those who are haunted by the amount of dust at home.

## THE SQUEEGEE CAN ALSO BE USED ON ITS OWN

When Auri's friend Anni did not adopt the combination of a microfiber towel and a squeegee despite her best efforts, Auri advised her to try the dryer dry, just like that. The same trick is used by Auri's mother, who often uses the dryer dry at home, as it collects dog hair well, in particular. A bit like the way a rubber spatula or window squeegee removes loose dirt from carpets and sofas.

A squeegee is therefore equally suitable for use on its own. There is no need to be afraid of scratching, since its rubberized material does not create pressure on the floor.

## Repeller of Hated Dust

Dust is such a peculiar guest that it knows how to go into hiding. Stains and stubbornness show their faces immediately, but the dust is more cunning than them. In numerous homes, the presence of dust is realized only when rays of sun fall into the room. The light from the window reveals dust particles floating slowly in the air like bodies in space. Thick dust deposits on top of surfaces or furniture.

Can the movement or accumulation of dust be somehow prevented? Auri has a short and non-consoling answer: no, it can't. Dust finds its way to the place, no matter how neatly and conscientiously a person lives. Dust is released from textiles, people themselves, and the outdoors, especially if you live in a city. The dustiest place in the house is often the bedroom, because it is there that people roll around in their sheets and store their clothes.

Actually, the only way to avoid dust would be to spend as little time at home as possible. On the other hand, dust is in the air

even when we have been traveling, i.e. away from home for up to several weeks. According to Auri, the most dust-free person is a person who has moved to the countryside far from the city, has only taken his or her necessary things with them, and uses textiles as little as possible. Few people have the opportunity, or even desire, for a similar lifestyle, so the presence of dust is acceptable.

Still, there's something for the dust. The main thing to remember, first of all, is that it is not worth starting the cleaning day with wiping dust. For example, if you are planning to wrap the bed in clean sheets on the same day, you should only wipe the dust after changing the sheet. The sheets raise dust in the air in the same way as a vacuum cleaner. This also applies to airing textiles or taking clothes to the laundry basket. That's why it's a good idea to take care of the other maneuvers before taking out the dust.

When it comes to wiping dust, the rule of thumb applies to go from top to bottom. First we wipe from above, then proceed in stages going lower until all the dust has certainly fallen all the way to the floor. From there, it can be easily picked up with the help of a squeegee and microfiber cloth. According to Auri, the method applies to all cleaning.

The microfiber towel does not disappoint when wiping dust. A common mistake is to use a towel when it is too damp. There are four options:

1. Dry towel, not using water at all.

2. A damp towel, in which case water is sprayed on the towel.

3. A damp towel that has been soaked thoroughly, but when you wipe with it, it does not leave droplets behind. And when it is squeezed, water does not drain from it. Auri's favorite!

4. A wet towel that gives off water around it. Actually, wiping wet is washing rather than wiping. It is not a very functional remedy against dust.

Many cleaners are frustrated by the presence of specks of dust, no matter how much you wipe. The reason may lie in a towel that is too wet. Although the towel should be damp, it should not be too wet for dust to stick to it. Auri knows that some people wipe dust even with the towel dry, so it does not give off dust and dirt, but keeps those particles inside it. She still prefers a damp surface on the towel, as it is more effective than dry. While a damp towel captures the dust, it also cleans stains.

Speaking of a microfiber towel, one cannot ignore the duster. That cinematic cleaning tool, often dyed in rainbow colors, with which old ladies in our imaginations fiddle with their chandeliers. The description is clichéd and helplessly one-sided, at least if you ask Auri. She appreciates the duster, as it extends over large areas. It wipes shelves, lamps, and the part of the air conditioning duct on the ceiling that is visible in the apartment, while making the air in the room fresher.

Actually, the duster works exactly the same as the microfiber towel used dry. The difference is that with it the apartment is dusted faster, thereby saving both muscles and time. So choose a damp towel rather than a dry towel, Auri would say if you asked. Dusters can work in two different ways: either collect or drop dust. For example, an ostrich-feathered one drops dust down, while a sheepskin and a microfiber one collect it in itself. Both types of dusters have their fans, and they are equally suitable for home cleaning. Perhaps the most significant and exciting fact is that dust gathers dust. If there is dust floating somewhere, it is certain that soon there will be more and more of it there. Because of this fact, Auri admits that she dreamed of a cleaning tool made of dust. The bunnies hiding under the bed are made of dust that has gathered friends with it, turning into rather large balls. They attract each other.

"An already dusty instrument would be amazing," Auri sums up.

## A Forty-Five Minute Cleaning Day

What do Auri's visits to bomb-prone homes, the cleaning tips she shares, and her endless love of cleaning have in common? The answer is simple: flexibility. It's the ultimate magic word for how cleaning became Auri's greatest passion. Even the competence and confidence accumulated over the years—knowing what you are doing and what works for what—does not beat flexibility.

When the attitude is flexible and gentle, cleaning does not develop into a duty that pounds in the head as demanding. Auri carries that attitude with her in many situations. When she cleans up the bomb homes, she has to leave them unfinished, without a perfect outcome. When she distributes cleaning tips, she stresses that it is not necessary to try them all if certain dirty spots do not bother the residents themselves. And when Auri cleans her home, she only does so when and as she pleases.

The flexible attitude and the fact that she doesn't even try to eliminate dirt and clutter from the world also makes Auri a spur-of-the-moment cleaner. It may take thirty seconds, but it's cleaning up, just as much as a more in-depth session would be.

There are a lot of spontaneous inspirations like that in Auri's everyday life. In addition to them, once a week, she does a checkup cleaning. In other words, you look around properly and then choose what to do. In general, it is a quick wipe of the floor where there is dirt, not the meticulous nitpicking of every corner. For Auri, the rush of cleaning does not mean that, for example, a floor that looks clean must be wiped completely. It often involves cleaning the sinks, but if they look clean, Auri might just sweep the bathroom floor with a squeegee and shake the carpet.

For Auri, the purpose of cleaning is to maintain the home nicely enough for her own eyes. For some, it makes the chore easier to set the start time for cleaning. adjust the alarm to turn on after a quarter of an hour, and then do everything you can in that time, but no more. In this way, one will embrace quick cleaning and, in due course, enjoy its fruits. Maybe you realized how much you can do with short-term cleaning. Suddenly, cleaning isn't a bogeyman lurking on a day off.

Auri has often reserved a slice, or even a larger notch, from her Sunday for cleaning. Not because the home is actually screaming for cleaning in distress, but because cleaning is Auri's quality time. It's like a new episode of a favorite series or a hobby that's been burning in your back pocket all week long, and you're finally going to get to work on it at the end of the week. Sunday may be long awaited by many people. When Auri wakes up in the morning, she doesn't think about what she needs to clean up, but what she would like to clean up. In all likelihood, Sunday will go something like this:

1.  It all starts with dust, if it is not necessary to change the sheets. Dust whip in your hand and go. If you have the energy, you can wipe the same surfaces with a microfiber towel.

2.  Monitor kitchen cleaning. It involves wiping the doors with a microfiber towel and dishwashing detergent, washing the sinks with the same substances and checking the kitchen cabinets. The cutlery cabinet can also be cleaned with a familiar mixture of dishwashing detergent and rinsing thoroughly.

3.  Next is the bathroom. First, Auri turns her attention to the contact points, i.e. wipes the door handles with a microfiber towel. After that, she washes the sink with either an acidic or alkaline detergent. The same treatment is also applied to the toilet, first on the outside and finally on the inside. Lastly, Auri empties the trash, fills the toilet paper storage, and wipes the floor. Sometimes she cleans both toilets in the home, sometimes just the upstairs restroom that is in heavy use.

4.  Now it is the turn of the stairs of the home. Instead of vacuuming, Auri walks down them with a duster. She digs out the vacuum cleaner if the carpets need to be deep-cleaned or the furniture ventilated.

# CHAPTER 6

# IT'S OVER!
## *Or Not.*

Auri is able to do her home cleaning routine in less than forty-five minutes if she wants to, but it's rarely enough for her. More typically, cleaning stretches into a multi-hour or day-long experience. Sometimes Auri washes the windows, other times she changes the sheets or goes through the wardrobe. On holidays, she adds spice to the routine, such as wiping the walls and ceiling on a ladder and moving the cabinets aside so that even the places under them can be cleaned.

Even if it takes less than an hour to clean up, for Auri, the moment brings the same kind of excitement as a full-day scramble. It's easy to get into the hustle and bustle when the apartment never looks finished, like it should somehow be processed in advance to be cleanable. There is no need to clean before cleaning. Let's not rearrange the debris in new places, or clear it out of the way and out of sight for a while. At whatever point Auri stops cleaning, the home will not remain unfinished. Her forehead vein doesn't throb to indicate that she still feels uncomfortable with the half-finished state. Even if, for example, she threw a microfiber towel into the wash halfway through the project, the home would not be in an unwelcome jam. In order to make sense of cleaning, Auri encourages you to first attend to what feels most alarming at any given moment. What's the most annoying thing about the house's lack of cleanliness?

## Finally

Someone else would have already gotten bored and changed direction. That's what I think when I watch Auri's pace from the sidelines. Her everyday life could certainly be lived more easily than Auri lives it; she travels several hours a week to clean homes for free. She arrives home from home, carries garbage bags, and arranges things, and soon repeats the same thing.

Auri wouldn't be forced to succumb to the stinking rumble time and time again, at least not as often as she does, if she didn't want to do it. In a way, the everyday life of a cleaning star reminds me of the life of a touring artist. Every week, the target is a new apartment, where some stranger lives. A bit like the artist, Auri takes over a new place and a new audience, a new person, every week.

Like band members, Auri often sleeps in hotels while at multi-day cleaning gigs. We drive to the places in a van, which is like a miniature tour bus. Sometimes Anni, Santeri, a cousin, or someone else sits next to her, but it is very likely that Auri will go on the highway alone. Britney Spears's music or the voice of a grandma, mother, or journalist on the phone accompanies her.

For Auri, a hotel night doesn't mean tampering with what the minibar has to offer, wrapping herself in a thick blanket and a breakfast stretched into brunch. It's about choosing the hotel closest to the cleaning site indiscriminately, sometimes ending up in a luxury high-rise, sometimes a dump. When she gets to her room, she falls into bed like a rag after an average of seven hours of cleaning. At six in the morning, she once again puts her Apple watch on her wrist, munches on breakfast, drives the car back to the target, and cleans the bomb home again from morning till night. When it's clean enough, Auri can hop into her van again and drive back to Tampere. And the following week, the rumble repeats again, for the umpteenth time, and I don't think there's an end to the rumble.

After being at the gig, I can be sure of one thing: if the only prize for the eternal cleaning drumbeat was a video that gathered millions of views, it wouldn't last very long. Auri's exceptional affection for cleaning can't be denied, but there must be some deeper reason for it.

While chatting with Auri and spying on her at a cleaning gig, I've been trying to come to grips with something I feverishly believe exists. Why do people think she does this work? The urge to help those in need and earn virtue points? To gather overwhelming admiration and fans? To be constantly on the road, at home and abroad, and to get to places that others cannot reach? Put your brain in the cloakroom, take a break from everyday life, and forget about the demanding beeping email and all the earthly surroundings for a couple of days? Well, if truth be told, I don't believe in any of the options listed above.

Instead, I believe that it is symbolically a blast. Yep, it sounds rough, but that's probably what it's all about, even in that love of cleaning. It is about the desire to clear up the surrounding reality, to come and take over the space. To see how a one-woman whirlwind brings about a miniature revolution. To show others, but above all to herself, that she is the best in the world at what she does. And in order for the inexorable truth not to be forgotten, to expire, or even to flare up, the claim must be proven true every single week. Of course, there is another way to prove or keep that strong claim alive month after month and year after year.

Finally, I am forced to acknowledge one more thing. I still can't cope with the mess, especially the supposedly lovely rubbish and dust that dots the floors. They make me uneasy even when I've already been with Auri clearing Osku's floor in plain sight.

I still get annoyed when gravel, crumbs of food, leaves that have fallen from trees, and dust balls from the floor get stuck to the socks, adventuring from socks to the couch and finally to the bed. Even though I insisted beforehand that I wouldn't get frustrated with the little things after a cleaning gig with Auri, it wasn't long before I was on my former quest for a fanatically clean floor. When rubbish and dust take over the house as if in an unspoken agreement, I'm used to them being a sign of a home screaming for a thorough day of cleaning, expecting that they lock me and my co-occupants inside the four walls until it's clean enough. I have refused to believe that you could just attack a pile of rubble for five minutes and then let it be. But now, like any radical in her own life, I'm trying it. I remove the sweeping brush from the closet and use it to loosen dirt and stains on the floor, my weak spot. I enjoy it when small dots and swirls disappear from the floor effortlessly. Then I dump my prey in the bin and stop. Was that trivial moment really cleaning up? Can I say I cleaned up today if someone asks? Yes it is and yes you can, she said when I ask her about it. Auri vows to bring me a squeegee the next time she sees me. After that, I'll reportedly wait for the floor to be wiped like a child waiting for candy, she promises. I'll see, I'll smile. Even if the cleaning equipment is changed, I really do have a journey into that Auri mentality where you can mess up your home in order to clean it.

I know Auri isn't one of those people who tell guests to take off their shoes at the door and watch out for stains on the tablecloth. She doesn't flinch when frying oil splashes on the hood, or the face cream leaves its greetings on the bathroom mirror. On the contrary: Auri hopes, almost prays, for dirt to arrive. And yet Auri is also the type who doesn't bother to make her bed, because an unmade bed doesn't hurt. Auri's wardrobe, it would be an abomination for someone who loves absolute order. She can't handle folding her clothes. The other country was Sami's shirts, as they are larger, rectangular, and therefore more fun to scythe through. But with your own closet, it can always be messed up, it doesn't hurt at all.

This is where I think of all my cabinets. There are slips of paper and flags hiding inside the desk, which, in their chaos, remind me of our cleaning gig. My wardrobe, where you can't take out a blouse without the rest of the fashion creations on that shelf following as a slide. My dry goods cabinet, where packages like microwave popcorn, oatmeal, and juice concentrate hang out in perfect harmony, just messed-up.

When I started writing this book, I thought that, while refining the end credits, I would have learned to be ashamed of my cabinets and arrange them in a condition worthy of an interiors magazine.

But how is it? Now I find myself in an absurd situation where I look at the cupboards approvingly and assure them that Auri would not judge them either. As long as the systematization does not bother me, they are allowed to continue as it is.

I, on the other hand, focus with a clear conscience on those pain points in the home that bring rage to the brink. On that dirty floor, for example.

Auri, if anyone, is also the type who willingly gives tips if asked for advice on cleaning. Still, Auri can't say what's appropriate, what's too much, and what's mercilessly little cleaning. The answer to the question is, as boring as it may sound, in the person themself. In other words, we have to accept our own and each other's notions of cleanliness. Absolution belongs to everyone: those who are lustful, those who are used to or struggling with their mess, and everyone in between. The essence of Auri's love of cleaning does not spring from the worship of clean and tidy homes. It doesn't get a spark from the tormenting homesickness, from our condemnation of each other's homes—or, most horribly, each other based on our homes.

We must accept that one gets anxious about things, the other about dirt, and the third about nothing. We do not clean and will not continue to do so according to the same, deadly well-defined formula. Cleaning cannot fit into the world of correctly filling in Kela notes or following the directions for use of medicine. One may be able to be taught if the other person asks for it, but it cannot and does not need to be forced. In the end, everyone cleans how they like, or they don't clean until the clean dishes run out and the dust starts to become a presence.

The illusion of necessity, if anything, waters down the love of cleaning like a wet rag. The idea that you have to clean up, or that you have to clean up like someone else. And when you come home after a day at work, there's the housework lurking there, which you simply have to do and perform.

In some homes, people argue, fight, and cry about cleaning. After all, we will soon suffocate here when healthy indoor air goes and peace of mind goes with it. After all, we lose our sanity when things are scattered in the rooms and cannot find their right place. It's a must to clean up here, or else, we might think. Is it really so? How do you have to, why do you have to? As someone who has cleaned up a bomb room, Auri would say that the real necessity or obligation to clean is only extremely rare, in exceptional cases. More often than not, it's about what we've gotten ourselves used to.

So what? If cleaning is frustrating, is it the antidote to stop cleaning altogether? Or just start using a different kind of language? Instead of having to clean up, you would say you can clean if you feel like it. Ding-dong, and you're in love with cleaning, and a potential family on the side. Everyone knows that simply changing the verb will not solve it, but this is Auri's first cleaning tip. Want to hear the rest? Like it or not, here they come:

## The Seventeen Cleaning Commandments

*(In Random Order)*

1. Don't talk about cleaning like everyone else. Instead of having to clean up, try a revolutionary way of speaking: you get to clean up.

2. Deliberately make the cleaning day and the meanings loaded into it so wonderful that you can really wait for it to arrive. Put your favorite music on full stereo, or immerse yourself in an interesting audiobook. Clean together, and above all as a team. How about having a playful cleaning contest and seeing who is faster? Or throw some stuff away, because it makes you feel bubbly, and cleaning starts to taste like something other than wood. It also works that you plan in advance what delicacy you are going to pick up in the store or order *after* cleaning. And hey, would a moment of indulgence or a movie night in a clean home be anything? Don't forget to juice up about what good exercise cleaning is. By cleaning, you always do good for your body, mind, and home.

3. Get rid of excess stuff. The less stuff there is to move around and organize, the more fun (and easier) cleaning will be.

4. Think about the cleaning order before you start. Believe it or not, that alone speeds things up and makes them a lot more efficient.

5. Go one technique at a time and one room at a time. So do not first empty the table in the hall and wipe it, then wash the sinks in the kitchen, and then... No! Instead, first clear everything that needs to be cleared. Wipe everything you need to wipe at once. After that, clean everything that needs cleaning. Repeat this in every room. When you do one thing for as long as you can, you don't waste time shuttling between instruments and technology.

6. Forget the Adamant phrase about how to proceed from the purest to the dirtiest. Be reformist and only clean up dirty places. They give you guaranteed satisfaction. If you're left with a cleaning tooth, you can continue to less dirty places with loose wrists, as the most crucial game moves have been made.

7. Give all the credit to the hustling cleaning. Give up the all-or-nothing mentality. You really don't always have to clean everything and everywhere. To clean up, a few minutes of toilet cleaning is also counted. And that's not all: just washing the sink counts as cleaning, and you don't have to clean the entire toilet.

8. Do not forcibly rub the stain, but rather give it time. Time is the cleaner's undervalued, overshadowed bestie, as it softens even the hardest-headed dirt in the end. Spray the substance and leave it to brew.

9. Practice cleaning techniques. It's worth it. When you learn, for example, how to fold a microfiber towel correctly, the outcome is perfection, and you save a lot of time.

10. Don't get bogged down in dirty or broken cleaning equipment. Cleaning is a 100 percent equipment sport. If the towel is dirty, wash it, don't go around with a dirty rag. Otherwise, it will spread dirt around. Respect the towel and it will work the way you want it to work.

11. Replace the vacuuming with the squeegee. You will save time, your ears and your blood pressure, but the end result will be the same.

12. Try a timer. Only clean as much or as little as you can within the predetermined time. You might be surprised at what you can do in a quarter of an hour.

13. Clean up for yourself and nothing more. Does someone visiting criticize your chaos-ridden shoe shelf, which couldn't hurt you less? In one ear and out the other. Or does your friend or mother praise the power of the bathroom tile seams, the ones you can't really clean yourself, in a slightly suggestive tone? Thank them for the tip as adults do and then let the seams rest in peace. They don't exist for your friend or mom.

14. If cleaning a place seems tedious or laborious, try changing the technique. Usually, the lack of fluency is due to the fact that the task is handled too precisely or simply incorrectly.

15. Bet on quality and not quantity. The wallet will also thank you. You can get by with surprisingly little: hand dishwashing detergent, acidic agent (such as vinegar), cleaning stone, microfiber towel, cleaning blade, dish brush, dust spray, sponge, and squeegee. If they're lurking in your cleaning closet, you're already actually invincible.

16. Enjoy what you have done. Take pictures of the starting point and the final result. Feel the mood with how you manage your home, not the other way around. You decide where the dirt is going to spin and when that same dirt gets permission to fade. As is known about Auri's cleaning gigs, no power mess in the world beats the hand of a skilled human cleaner.

17. Love the mess. If the home is never overwhelmed by rumbles and mounds, even the euphoria after cleaning will shrink into a faint spill under the chest. In a word, even if the truth happens: when you learn to love not cleaning, you will also find a love of cleaning.

# ABOUT THE CONTRIBUTORS

## About the Author

Oona Laine (born in 1996) is a lifestyle journalist working at Helsingin Sanomat, the largest newspaper in the Nordic countries. She graduated with a master's degree in media and communication from the University of Helsinki.

## About Auri Kananen

Auri Kananen is a professional cleaner and a cleaning influencer. She rose to fame with her TikTok cleaning videos; since then she has gained over nineteen million followers across her social media platforms.

## About the Translator

Nea Mattila is Auri's editor and assistant. They have been working together since 2021. Nea is an engineering student and a mom of one. She is fluent in English and was therefore asked by Auri to translate this book.

Mango Publishing, established in 2014, publishes an eclectic list of books by diverse authors—both new and established voices—on topics ranging from business, personal growth, women's empowerment, LGBTQ+ studies, health, and spirituality to history, popular culture, time management, decluttering, lifestyle, mental wellness, aging, and sustainable living. We were named 2019 *and* 2020's #1 fastest growing independent publisher by *Publishers Weekly*. Our success is driven by our main goal, which is to publish high-quality books that will entertain readers as well as make a positive difference in their lives.

Our readers are our most important resource; we value your input, suggestions, and ideas. We'd love to hear from you—after all, we are publishing books for you!

Please stay in touch with us and follow us at:

Facebook: Mango Publishing
Twitter: @MangoPublishing
Instagram: @MangoPublishing
LinkedIn: Mango Publishing
Pinterest: Mango Publishing
Newsletter: mangopublishinggroup.com/newsletter

Join us on Mango's journey to reinvent publishing, one book at a time.